In My Father's Footsteps

W. W. NORTON & COMPANY   NEW YORK LONDON

In My Father's Footsteps

A MEMOIR

SEBASTIAN MATTHEWS

For information about permission to reproduce selections from this book,
write to Permissions, W. W. Norton & Company, Inc., 500 Fifth Avenue,
New York, NY 10110

Manufacturing by the Haddon Craftsmen, Inc.

Book design by Chris Welch

Production manager: Julia Druskin

Library of Congress Cataloging-in-Publication Data

Matthews, Sebastian, date.

In my father's footsteps / by Sebastian Matthews.—1st ed.

p. cm

ISBN 0-393-05738-0 (hardcover)

1. Matthews, Sebastian, date. 2. Matthews, Sebastian, date.—Family. 3.
Matthews, William, 1942– 4. Poets, American—20th century—Biography. 5.
College teachers—North Carolina—Asheville—Biography. 6. Asheville
(N.C.)—Biography. I. Title.

CT275.M4645516A3 2004

975.6'88—dc21

2003018195

W. W. Norton & Company, Inc.

500 Fifth Avenue, New York, N.Y. 10110

www.wwnorton.com

W. W. Norton & Company Ltd.

Castle House, 75/76 Wells Street, London W1T 3QT

1 2 3 4 5 6 7 8 9 0

for Ali

in memory of my father

Contents

Crossing the Threshold

First they take it away,
for now the body belongs to the state.
Then they open it
to see what may have killed it,
and the body had arteriosclerosis
in its heart, for this was an inside job.

WILLIAM MATTHEWS, "My Father's Body"

WHEN THE OFFICER stepped back, I was the first to pass through the broken police seal. Ali, my wife, came in close behind me. The young cop followed. The older cop brought up the rear, closing the heavy door behind him. For a moment, the four of us huddled at the start of the long, dimly lit hall. Down at the end of the passageway, where it made a sharp left, the light from the guest room window dropped onto the worn carpet in an elongated rectangle. The apartment was unsettlingly quiet.

The older cop walked down the hallway, turning on lights as he went, first in the bathroom, then in my father's bedroom. His partner trailed after him, posting sentry at the guest room door. A cat scurried out from under his feet, disappearing in a blur of fur around the corner. This kick-started Ali, who drifted from my side and entered my father's study. I stood in place, stunned.

The night before, I had called my father from Ann Arbor to wish him a happy fifty-fifth birthday. A strange voice came on the line. *That's not my father.*

I said: "Bill Matthews, please."

Ali looked up from her book.

"Who is this?" the voice said.

"This is his son. Who's *this?*"

A pause, then: "This is Officer O'Hara. I am sorry to have to inform you, but your father, William Matthews, passed away earlier this evening."

The phone seemed limp in my hands. Ali was at my side, an expectant look on her face that wanted to transform into a smile.

"He's dead. My dad's dead."

AFTER A LONG night of calls to family and friends, after frantic packing and planning, we had caught a late morning flight out of Detroit International to JFK. We dropped off our luggage at the hotel, pausing long enough to call the on-duty detective. He told us to take a taxi to my father's Upper West Side apartment; a uniformed escort would be waiting. In the lobby, the older of the two policemen, a sleepy-eyed Irishman, told us what we already knew:

"You're only allowed access into the deceased's apartment for ten, fifteen minutes. I'm not supposed to let you take anything out. Just the necessary clothes for the funeral—and the will, if there is one. Clear?"

Because my father had officially died alone, the detective had told us, a court order would have to be procured before we could gain permanent access to his residence. In accordance with state law, the police had placed a seal across the door, to remain until we appointed an estate administrator, navigated the court system, obtained the proper forms. Then, and only then, could the police escort the "bereaved" back to the "deceased's" apartment and allow us inside. It would take a few days, maybe as long as a week.

As the elevator made its way up to the fifth floor, I had tried to imagine what we would find in the apartment. They didn't make chalk outlines for natural deaths, did they? Would his computer still be on, coffee cold in the cup? I couldn't do it. Instead, I pictured Dad in his morning routine, slouched on the couch in his ratty flannel robe, busy reading the *New York Times*. He'd be nodding his head to the jazz seeping out of the deck as he sipped the hot coffee and his cat, Velcro, purred out sutras at his feet. All I wanted was to join them there, up late from a hard sleep. The whole ride up, the younger officer, a handsome, square-jawed Latino, stared at his reflection in the mirrored glass.

Now that we were actually inside the apartment, I didn't know what to do. I peered uneasily through the open study door. My father's literary papers were strewn on his desk, books scattered on the floor: stacks of hardcovers weighed down the side table, a hodgepodge of reader's copies, students' first books, uncracked novels. His tape deck perched on a bookshelf next to the mammoth, open Webster's dictionary. The familiar mother-and-child Picasso print hung by the window alongside a framed ink drawing of two Japanese monks glaring at each other like Laurel and Hardy. His black leather chair stalled in the center of the room, empty.

Ali was thumbing through desk drawers and gathering manila folders into a pile. I wanted to tell her to stop, to remind her that my father was an intensely private man: that rifling through his stuff was the equivalent of pickpocketing. But I didn't say anything. I wanted more time to take everything in. His tattered leather jacket hanging on the coatrack. The umbrellas and walking sticks leaning against each other in the corner. The bulletin board with its collage of old postcards.

Standing there in the hall, I became overwhelmed by his undeniable presence, by the olfactory amalgam of dust, mold, and stale cigarette smoke that made up his living space. Momentarily transported back to high school, I was once again in our big, empty Seattle house. Walking up the stairs to deliver a fresh cup of French Roast to my father, hunched over his Selectric, smoking. Met at the turn by the subtle undercurrent of his body odor—nutmeg, sweat, Grey Flannel cologne, essence of old sweater.

They said my father died in the bathroom, collapsing of a heart attack while dressing for the opera, dead before his body slid to the floor. That his girlfriend, Celia, was let in by the doorman and found him. (It was she who would come and fetch the cat.) I didn't look into that room, focusing, instead, on the floor-to-ceiling wall of poetry books that loomed before me on my left. I came to a full stop before the huge library of slim, dusty volumes; it was like being in front of a gigantic beehive, or a bank of computers. A massive amount of stored energy pulsated in front of me. Running my finger over the spines of the hardcovers (Stevens' *Collected*, Berryman's *Dream Songs*, Pound's *Cantos*, Baudelaire's *Les Fleurs du Mal*), I marveled at the sheer magnitude of the collection, the weight of all the words.

The broadsides lining the opposite wall seemed lit up from within, the hand-set poems shining in their frames. It felt like I had slipped into a museum after hours and was passing alone through a library's special collection room, a hall of cases and frames containing undecipherable, heraldic mysteries. Before me:

the immortalized life of the poet—printed on museum-quality paper, bound and displayed in glass frames, embossed with illustrations and calligraphic signatures. As though I was trespassing on my legacy.

I MOVED FORWARD. The door to the bedroom hung open, its crooked frame calling me onto its threshold. The room was shrouded in darkness, blinds pulled down. My father's immense bed, which took up most of the room, floated in the dark. I thought back to all the moments when I'd stood in the doorway and watched him nap, face down in the pillow, feet draped over the side. *Dad*, I'd whisper, *time to wake up*. What would happen if I stretched out—then and there—in my father's sleep imprint? Would I feel the last echo of his heartbeat?

Of course, none of this was going to help. I couldn't stay in this room; nor was I ready to select the clothes for the burial. That chore would have to wait. It was as if I had been placed on a moving sidewalk, against my will, and now couldn't step off. All of a sudden out of breath, I turned for the door, panicky in the cramped room. But the young cop was standing at the bend in the hall, blocking my path into the living room. After a brief standoff, he moved out of my way.

The living room shades were pulled down and the lights were on bright, making the usually warm and shady space feel empty and cold. Ali was now in the back room; I could hear her opening cabinets and drawers. Street noise wafted in through the windows: cars moving through their gears and schoolchildren at recess calling to each other in play. In a trance, I turned off the lights, opened the blinds, and watched as the afternoon sunlight rushed to its familiar spot on the floor. This was only a minor improvement.

When a pigeon flew up past the window, its shadow slithering over the red brick buildings across the way, a melody started playing in my head—one of those slow-starting Monk compositions that winds itself up like a hand-cranked record player. The first melody was followed by other fragments of song, by little snippets of music I'd listened to in this room over the years. Cuts off Miles' *Kind of Blue*. Marley's chanting on *Babylon by Bus*. The anguished cry in *Rigoletto*. A running rush in a Mozart sonata. The opening climb of Bach's first cello suite. Dylan's "You're Gonna Make Me Lonesome When You Go."

And then I was lost, back at all the dinner parties my father held for his literati friends. Elegant people milling about. Bottles of wine opened and emptied in a spontaneous toast of glasses. My father holding court in the center of a small group, wineglass in hand, left leg splayed out in front of him, right wrist curled back against his waist, elbow out. Leaning back a little, eyes sparkling, he surveyed his audience before letting loose his trademark wit. It was as though he was surfing: the board he crouched on was his sharp mind, the wave the tumult of words forming inside him. People were leaning in, either curious bystander or comrade in-the-know. And a pretty young woman had moved intently into my father's sphere, placing her hand on his arm. She was looking up at him, wanting to know everything she could about this man.

Dust particles danced in the air. The tenant upstairs was dragging something heavy across the floor. I stood in place, breathing slowly, aware of the dropped ballast of my hands. My *dad is dead*.

M y father went to the post office the morning of his death. He loved sending letters, enjoyed the whole routine of correspondence. He liked licking the stamps, separating out the envelopes he knew by feel took more than the standard postage, trudging to the post office for sheets of stamps. He even got something out of waiting in line. He dug the simple anonymity of it; how, standing patiently in the passage of dead time, he could dream up lines of poetry under the high ceilings.

I imagine him walking down Amsterdam Avenue, stopping briefly at the used-book cart to scan titles, then passing by the dreary entrance to St. Luke's Hospital. After his turn at the STAMPS ONLY window, he crosses over the Columbia campus and walks slowly back up Broadway. He is happy to be out walking again: the procedure to clean out the arteries in his legs has given him back his mobility. Maybe he picks up some dry cleaning or stops in at the grocery on 115th for a few additions to that night's risotto— fresh basil, pine nuts, portobellos.

When he was still a smoker, he'd have made a quick pit stop at the corner market, stuffing the cigarette packs in his coat pockets on his way out. By the next corner, he'd have the first packet open and a fresh cigarette between his fingers. But he had quit smoking at this point, and the mechanics of that lifelong habit had slowly faded. (I used to like watching him light up, for I could see just how much he enjoyed the act of smoking. The need must have been at its greatest before the replenishment of his supply, of course, but it was more than that. He loved opening the pack, shaking out the smoke; loved bending over the match, then standing back up into himself. He reveled in taking that first drag, which he always seemed to do while looking off in the distance. In those moments he seemed both beautifully preoccupied and intensely focused.)

I can remember going out to dinner with him the winter before the surgery, and the excruciating walk to one of his favorite neighborhood spots. He stopped literally every block to rest, lighting up a cigarette to cover his fatigue, using awkward flourishes of small talk to fill in the gaps. When we were finally settled in our seats and Dad's color had returned, he started fussing with the wine menu, and I had to pretend nothing out of the ordinary had happened. I did insist on flagging down a taxi for the ten blocks home, though. Relieved, he folded his tall, stiff body into the backseat.

I've always felt that he used those neighborhood walks as a way to nudge his poetic faculties—the little jaunts through the day set his mind in motion. And I like to imagine that he was hot on the trail of a new poem that last morning. How on the way back home he followed the parabolic hump of Broadway as it flowed over 116th, passed Barnard College and Teachers College, Riverside Church in view, and began its ascent into the ever-receding boundaries of Harlem. Once back in his building, standing in the newly renovated elevator, he'd have been raring to go. Inside the apartment, his foot out to block the cat from escaping, he'd have dropped off the mail on his desk and headed for the kitchen to brew more coffee. Senses revived, he'd return to his study.

First, he'd tend to a few things, write notes to friends on the odd collection of postcards he'd gathered over the years. Then he'd start in on the poem itself, slowly, carefully, tinkering with the opening line, which had been stuck in his head since he was in the post office. (" 'Keep it under your hat,' the saying went") Hovering over it for a moment. Tapping the nib of the pen softly on the paper. ("when we wore hats.") Then leaning in and letting the poem unreel on the page.

Of course, I can only imagine all this. I can't know what actually happened that morning. Can't slip into my father's head. But as his son, as a fellow writer, I know my father's routines. I can picture that morning clearly in my mind's eye: a little snippet of film flickering on this screen.

So it's no surprise that my father wrote me a postcard the morning of his death. He sent one to my brother as well. They went in with the last batch of mail deposited at the post office. (John, a longtime doorman at the Spenser Apartments, remembers holding the door open for him on his way out.) I didn't receive the card until over a week after the funeral, not until we arrived back home in Ann Arbor. More than a little creepy to have the card fall out of the unruly stack of bills, catalogues, and letters.

The note was straightforward enough, written in his trademark handwriting: tight and crabby, tilted a bit, ending with "Love, Dad." Just a little heads up that he was back in town after a reading. The poet, happy after a hard year of bad health; the solitary man, sending out cards to his sons telling them where he was and that he loved them. The advertisement on the postcard was what set the hair on the back of my neck on end.

It was one of those thick-stock promotions you get in the bathrooms of Manhattan restaurants. This one was for ABC's new lineup of Wednesday night comedies. On a bright yellow background, in an old-fashioned typewriter font, the tag line read:

Laughter is the best medicine. Unless you're really sick.
Then you should call 911.

⤳

A YEAR BEFORE my father died, his doctor told him that he'd be dead by sixty if he didn't stop smoking. So finally, after three decades of heavy smoking, he quit cold turkey. From two packs a day to nothing. Then he went in for surgery to clean out arteries that had needed the attention years before.

The plan had been that my grandmother, Mary, would fly in from Newcastle, England, to care for her son the first few days after the operation. Ali and I would fly in around the time that his sister, Susan, was returning from an overseas trip. Together, we'd manage his informal nursing care. But, in typical Matthews fashion, both my father and my grandmother downplayed the severity of the operation. When Mary called with the news that things had gone poorly, I didn't know what to think. One moment she was assuring me that everything was okay, that I didn't need to come, the next she was crying and saying that my father had nearly died on the operating table.

I was working on the social staff at Bread Loaf, a writers' conference held for two weeks in August in the mountains above Middlebury, Vermont. Having first visited my father there as a teen, I had continued going through the years, heading up the mountain each summer to get my dose of its grand, heady romance. I had been a guest contributor, then a working scholar—paying my dues by waiting tables—and was now helping put together cocktail parties before dinner and pouring drinks for the faculty at night.

Ali was up visiting. We were calling New York every few hours to check on my father's condition. Luckily, my dad's best friend was at the conference visiting his wife, one of the poets on staff. It felt good to be part of a network of family and friends. After years of enduring my father's little secrets—his propensity to keep those who loved him in different compartments of his life—it was a relief to all be finally talking with one another. It was this friend who finally took me aside and told me to get down to New York.

He said: "I don't care what your grandmother says. He's your father. He's in trouble and he needs you. It's what sons do."

DAD LOOKED AWFUL. The surgery had lasted nearly eight hours. The doctors had to go in a second time when his extremities suddenly went cold, so he was postsurgery groggy, still trapped under an umbra of anesthesia when Ali and I arrived. My grandmother met us outside my father's room, her usually bright eyes tired and ringed with fear. She seemed profoundly relieved that we were there. Dad woke up just long enough to recognize us, trying for a moment and failing to put on a brave face. He quickly fell back asleep.

That first night I stayed with my father was the worst. One of the nurses found an extra cot, but I only managed a few fitful hours of sleep on its slippery plastic surface. Mostly I spent the night helping him out of bed and across the cold floor so he could throw up into the sink. His body was tinged gray, his skin droopy. The room smelled of sweat, released anesthetic, camphor, urine, and barely suppressed fear. Nurses drifted in and out like movie extras.

The next morning was equally rocky, with Dad throwing up some more and me frantically trying to track down the doctor. By noon things had evened out a little. He let the nurses prop him up on pillows, and though he looked pale and old, he cracked an easy joke about the hospital food. Some of the color had returned to his face. He seemed especially happy to see Ali and, after a few shy moments, even let her help him out of bed. Ali was a trained social worker, so it made sense that she'd know how to put him at ease. She averted her gaze as she helped him to the bathroom. When the doctor finally showed up, making encouraging statements about blood sugar levels and positive enzyme results, we unleashed relieved smiles, trying not to allow our anxiety to show.

Over the next four days, Ali and I shuttled back and forth between the hospital room and my father's fifth-floor apartment. Mary cleaned the apartment and went shopping. It was the end of August, Manhattan was in the midst of one of its infamous heat waves, and, to top it off, the elevator in my father's building, already inoperable for months, would be out indefinitely. We were miserable, burdened by fear and lethargic from the humidity. The only consolation: we were helping my father slowly crawl his way out of the ditch of ill health he had fallen into.

The day finally came for him to be moved back into his apartment. Out of pride he refused to be carried on a stretcher (and, in this decision, I sided with him), insisting that he could manage the steps on his own. It was a matter of his regaining a measure of dignity. But "on his own" actually meant that Ali and I hauled him up five flights of marble steps, taking his full weight between landings. The whole affair took over an hour, and I was afraid he was going to die of heatstroke before we could get him settled in his bed.

It had dawned on me back at the hospital, as I saw my father hesitantly step into his clothes, that he was happy to be alive. It was a sober realization. Despite all his shortcomings, despite a decade-long refusal to stop smoking and tone down the drinking—maybe, in part, for these reasons—I loved the old man. The thought of losing him paralyzed me. And just like that, feelings of love and pity were quickly joined by red-hot anger. *Old man?* He was only fifty-three. How dare he be such a wreck! The accusation burned in my head like an ice cream headache. I had to step out into the hallway while he finished buttoning his shirt.

And on the way down to the parking lot, in the crowded hospital elevator, and along the sterile corridors, a corrosive anger bubbled in my stomach. *How could you? How could you have treated yourself so poorly?* I couldn't tell whether I meant "do this to *me*" or "do this to *yourself*." Probably a little of both. It was surprising to discover that there was enough anger to spread around.

Ali asked me about it later.

"What happened? I thought you were going to explode, your face was so red."

"I don't know. I just all of a sudden got mad. Incredibly fucking mad."

"Why do you think?"

"I don't know."

We had been heading back to my father's apartment after a

quick bite out. I stopped on the corner and watched the students stream out of the Columbia gates. They seemed in a hurry to get to the next event of their lives, heedless of harm and illness. The anger reignited. For a flash I was angry at Ali, wishing she'd leave me alone. *I can figure this out on my own!* Besides, I didn't want her to question my feelings, but make room for them. I was so full up with contradiction, had so many feelings about my father, that I didn't know how to begin articulating them. I wanted to talk about his incredible stubbornness: his inability to change a lifestyle that everyone knew was slowly killing him. How even after his own father's early death from a heart attack, he couldn't, or wouldn't, change his habits.

At the same time, I knew how intricately those habits were woven into the fabric of his creative life. I knew that the wine fueled the poetry, that nicotine and coffee were the longtime companions of his creative composition. Knew firsthand that it's not that easy to sidestep a mode of living. Still, I wanted to yell at him, wanted to ask him why he was doing this to himself. Why he felt so compelled to marry the women he slept with. *After three failed marriages and thirty years, couldn't you have figured it out?!* Then again, weren't those very excesses part of the romance of his charm?

"Your fifteen minutes are up. Time to go."

The young cop loomed in the doorway, one hand at his shoulder cupping the walkie-talkie, the other dangling ineffectually at his side. He wanted to rest the hand on his gun holster, I could tell, but was probably afraid of coming across as too aggressive. He was antsy, ready to escort me from the apartment if I didn't get moving.

But I was not budging. I wanted to remind him: "My father is dead. There is nowhere to go." Then a desperate idea came to me: a notion of what I could do next. Instead of looking for signs of my father's presence—which could be found everywhere and were therefore stripped of their meaning—I would scout out his absence. I'd search for clues, for a tangible record of his remaining life. Some proof of his life having slipped away. Some kind of sign.

Once I came to this realization, the evidence was everywhere—in the fold of the *New York Times,* in the pile of mail on the coffee table, and in the fresh grape rust at the bottom of a single, stained wineglass. In the Tommy Flanagan disc frozen in the player. I was following my nose. I came upon a damp coffee filter resting in the kitchen sink filled with old grounds. The refrigerator was stocked with a whole rap sheet of evidence—the jar of capers, the rock-hard block of moldy Italian cheese. I found an old jar of kumquats, whole-bean coffee in a folded-down bag, a quart of grapefruit juice gone bitter, what looked like leftover pasta, a dried-up mango. My father's very own domestic crime scene.

The couch in the living room had a permanent indentation where he used to sit. I rested there, pretending that he had not died, that he had simply walked out of his life, out for a stroll and would be back any moment. It was a miserable thing to do, child-ish and naïve, but I couldn't help it. *He will come back with a bag of croissants,* I told myself. *I mustn't touch anything until he returns.*

When the older cop started telling horror stories about how families squabble over the deceased's possessions, how the nicest people can turn into monsters, I pretended to listen, but all I could do was focus on the objects around me. The artwork on the walls, the racks of CDs, the books lying everywhere. I didn't want his stuff—I wanted to be left alone with it. All I wanted to do was to sit down and immerse myself in the slowly dying energy of the room.

To shut the cop out, I took up the stack of mail and began shuffling through the usual catalogues, bills, letters from friends and colleagues, literary magazines. In the middle of the pile, I came upon a letter addressed in my own handwriting. It was the birthday card I sent him a few days back. Unopened.

WHEN THE OLDER cop nodded to his impatient partner, I knew it was time to get to the business at hand. I forced myself to walk down the hall and enter the bedroom, wishing I had a face covering, some kind of grief mask to wear. Sidestepping the bed, I quickly opened the closet to the wardrobe of suits, pants, dress shirts. There were nearly a hundred ties. Dress shoes in a line along the floor. Piles of short-sleeve shirts still in their crisp dry-cleaning fold. It took me a while to choose an appropriate suit; I ended up going with the gray Armani. I didn't know which tie to choose so grabbed four or five. Trying to remember how he dressed at my wedding, not knowing whether to follow my taste or guess at his. Finally adding a white dress shirt, black leather shoes. He was dead for only a day, and I was already relying on memory to construct his image.

The cops started to escort me out, but I stopped at the bathroom, ready to confront whatever truth resided there. They seemed to understand. The senior officer took the clothes from me and backed up to let me pass, closing the door to allow me privacy.

There were signs of the night before on the bathroom tile. Blood-soaked tissues stuck on the toilet bowl, unflushed. Raindrops of blood marking the floor. A single rubber glove lay contorted in the corner, thrown off by the coroner or the emergency medic. The pervasive, elemental smell of cleanser. I moved over to the toilet and sat down, questions swarming around in my head. Did he really not feel anything, or did he have a second of recognition? Did he have time to cry out, "*Oh shit!*"? Was he afraid? Did he think of his sons, or of Celia, or of his mother alone in England? Did Velcro come running, confused by the fallen body, crouching with him near the tub, leaning into the discharged heat coming off his body?

Ali opened the door and peered in. Her look was rife with sadness, love, and anger. I forced a weak smile, then joined her in the hall. It was time to go. We moved forward slowly, but I had this nagging feeling that I was forgetting something, that maybe there was something I could do, a personal act I could accomplish that might relieve this feeling of helplessness.

I waited for the young cop to busy himself with the lights, then, pretending I'd forgotten my keys, made my way back into the living room. The mail on the table. That was it! I grabbed the birthday card off the top of the pile and slipped it into my winter coat. Then the compact disc in the player, placed back carefully in its case. These, I knew for sure, belonged to me.

Ali was stalled on the landing, burdened with an armload of files, my father's Rolodex stuffed awkwardly in her bag. I took back the suit of clothes from the cop and folded it over my arm. When the younger cop started to say something about Ali's not-so-secret stash, his partner quieted him. He turned his body to block the view. I stepped closer, wishing to hear my father behind the door— his breath as he turned the latch, his soft-shoe shuffle back to his study.

But then two hands applied a giant neon Band-Aid to the door. And the place closed up like a wound.

Song for My Father

We're made in the image
of each other and don't know it. How hard
we'll fight to keep that ignorance they had
yet to learn, and they had me as a teacher.

WILLIAM MATTHEWS, "The Generations"

THERE'S A PHOTO of my father I keep propped up alongside the other family photos. The picture was taken a few months before his death, a commissioned shot for the jacket of his last book of poems. In it, my father's handsome face is split in two as if by an invisible line. One side appears stoic, almost melancholy, deadly serious. The other half is all-knowing smirk and barely suppressed grin. His usually unruly hair looks washed and combed; he wears an open-necked dress shirt under one of his countless wool suits. His mustache is lopsided in its trademark droop. The pouches under his eyes lend him the haggard, deeply thoughtful look of an insomniac. In this image resides the wise poet-sage, the seasoned veteran. But beside this figure, sharing his visage, poses the impish boy—the curious small-town Ohio paperboy returning to the public library for more books.

It's a fitting portrait, really, for my father always seemed to me a bundle of contradictions—a "sad, happy man," as a close friend once described him. A walking oxymoron, simultaneously generous and greedy, open and secretive, gregarious and shy, well dressed and unkempt. A loyal friend who, in his own estimation, failed completely in marriage. A generous and beloved teacher who hit on his students. ("A lush and a lech," one student called him without a trace of malice.) A highbrow with friends in low places. A pack rat who threw things away. A wonderfully attentive father who could forget to put dinner on the table. An incredibly verbose, articulate, and witty conversationalist and writer who often struggled to tell his sons how much he loved them.

MY FATHER HAD good taste. He was also what you'd call a snob. He only cared for the best—in coffee, in wine, in clothes and furniture, in art and in music. An "aristocrat of the spirit," to use E. M. Forster's wonderfully archaic term. It wasn't really a status thing with him, though, more a compulsion—the particular obsessiveness of the tastemaker. He acquired new tastes the way children collect toys. He'd stumble into a new love and then, enthralled, learn as much as he could about his new passion—jazz, wine, skin diving, cooking, orchids, detective novels, Italian shoes, opera. It was the clarity that comes with excellence that my father sought out and admired. Along the way he'd become an expert.

When he started listening to opera seriously, for instance, he began compiling an extensive library of CDs. He got season tickets to the Met, studied various libretti, and read all the biographies. He even interviewed one of the famous tenors, Alfredo Kraus, on the variety of ways the master used, and maintained, his vocal instrument. He had done the same with jazz two decades before. What kept him from being insufferable was his innate love of low art as well as high. As big a basketball fan as an opera lover, he equally enjoyed an old James Bond film and the Godard flick at Film Forum. Beer burgers and bouillabaisse. Janis and jazz. Picture television's Frasier but with more dignity, a more subdued desire for elevated social standing, and a keener, more innate sense of the hip.

He studied wine in this way, as a connoisseur. (Read: He was a drinker.) There are countless Bill Matthews stories told by friends and students. I hear them whenever I join a particular gathering of writers. They are affectionate, nostalgic stories, told both as a way to evoke my father's memory and to remind the teller of his or her own special connection to the great man. Many of these stories involve Bill Matthews choosing the wine at a late night gathering, or Matthews amazing the dinner table with an eloquent monologue on the type of soil from such and such vineyard or the seasonal history of a particular year in Napa Valley. They often start, *How about that special cabernet we drank together in . . .*

One of my favorite stories comes from the poet Rick Jackson, who tells how my father came to Chattanooga several times ("most for decent money, once for nothing, once for pennies"). On each visit they'd make a wine run, but during parties at Rick's house the students would get into their wine. By midnight, the students would have drunk up their stock. This happened again and again no matter where they hid their stash. Finally, one September, he called Rick and said, "Save your good wine bottles." When my father arrived later that fall they bought the regular good wine, and then some cheaper stuff—not bad, just not great— which they hand-poured into the empties. They hid the bottles but in places where they had been found before, and then stashed the good stuff under Rick's bed. All through the night, the students kept smiling, thinking they had put one over on their professors.

EVER THE SENSUALIST, my father had the hand-to-eye coordination of an athlete but no true or lasting control over his body. He smoked and drank too much, indulged in rich foods. He never stretched before exercising, rarely warmed up. Nevertheless, in his prime, he was skilled at baseball (a catcher like his father), basketball, racquetball, softball, and tennis. As he got older and his untrained body gradually gave out on him, he starting dropping sports. One injury per. His knees went, his hip tightened. Then smoking took his wind. Tennis was the last game to go, and the one my father struggled the hardest to hold on to. I remember the last sad games of doubles where he had to stop after almost every point to catch his breath. He couldn't even bend down to retrieve the ball.

It was his sense of humor, his witty sense of irony, that stayed sharp. He could obsess over a pun for days and then, once he had it, drop it into a cocktail party exchange or bury the linguistic treasure inside a poem crafted solely for its inclusion. He was also famous among his friends and students for coming up with witty rejoinders and poison-tipped remarks on the spot.

The poet Sascha Feinstein tells the story of my father giving a reading at Lycoming College. As he walked to the podium after the introduction, the crowd applauding him, an elderly couple from the very back of the room stood up, walked slowly down the aisle, and exited through the door a few feet away from my father.

Perhaps the couple had expected a different lecture, Feinstein surmises. Maybe they had come for a movie. Whatever the reason, they walked out on the reading before it got started. My father turned to the audience and said with a grin, "How am I doing so far?"

One of his favorite subjects was the wretched necessity of academia, which he called "a sort of methadone program for the depressed." Another of his favorite topics was psychotherapy, which he submitted to diligently most of his adult life. ("One of us has a friend / whose analyst died in mid-session, / nondirective to the end," he writes in "Good Company." Later in the same poem, he focuses on marriage, admitting: "I use it to scare myself.") It helped that his humor was often self-deprecatory: though he laughed at his own jokes, the jokes were often at his expense.

There was something of Oscar Wilde in my father's tossed-off asides, with their linguistic inversions and ironic attacks on euphemism. "The purpose of sexual intercourse," he writes, "is to get it over with as slow as possible." Or, in his essay "Privacies," he can't help punning on the title word: "In the army is it better to be a 'private' in a barracks or a 'general' alone in his office?" I've been at readings where my father stops in the middle of a poem to ask why, when a poem comes to a particularly satisfying conclusion, the audience often breaks into a collective, hushed moan. He looks out at the crowd with a sly smile and remarks, "It sounds like a gerbil having an orgasm."

In JANUARY OF 1997, my father came out to Ann Arbor for a semester-long stint as the University of Michigan's writer-in-residence. He didn't actually live in Ann Arbor. He commuted once a week. Which is vintage Bill Matthews. He didn't want to give up his weekend opera tickets, his late night MSG-channel Knicks games, or his dinners out with friends. In short: his life. At the same time, he couldn't turn down the paycheck, the chance to see his son.

Ali and I had been married for nearly two years and were living in a bottom-floor apartment in a nice house a few blocks over from the football stadium. Ali was more than halfway through a Ph.D. in social work, and I was an adjunct at the University of Michigan. Dad would come into town for three days each week, staying in a room at the Michigan League. We'd meet for coffee at one of the local coffeehouses or at faculty cocktail parties where we'd hang out in the corner with drinks in hand talking sports. A few times he came over for dinner, but mostly we'd get together at a restaurant somewhere in town. I had gotten used to our pattern of long stretches of silence punctuated by brief visits; had grown accustomed to visiting him on my drives east or to sharing infrequent holidays with him and my grandparents. He had always been too busy, too preoccupied with his own life, for a full-fledged visit. This was special.

My father had recovered from the previous year's operation and was looking good—a bit puffed up from having stopped smoking, but alive in the eyes, happy and full in his face. The last six months of surgery and recovery, and the years leading up to it—with Dad smoking more and walking less, drinking more and sleeping less—had been quietly harrowing. Hanging out with him was like watching an existential pay-per-view. Matthews vs. Matthews. May the best vice win. But now he was moving around again, had even lost some of his potbelly. (There was talk of a hip operation to recover even more mobility.) His color was back. His hope, too, the most important thing.

Little things indicated to me that he had been scared by his ill health and was ready for something else. Always a moderately heavy wine drinker, he had started drinking less. (I could never tell how much Dad actually drank on a regular basis, only that he bought wine by the case and drank it nightly by the bottle.) He started eating more healthfully, cutting back on the butter and the red meat, and was beginning to exercise again. He was in good form.

It would be easy to say that my father had turned his life around. Old habits, it seemed, were shed overnight. It was there in the way he acted with Celia. The hugs and kisses they gave each other. The love looks. There was even talk of them getting married, of buying a house out of the city for weekends and summer getaways. Had the quintessential lonely, romantic man finally settled down? I found it hard to believe. Even though I was excited about this apparent sea change in his life, I couldn't help being a little skeptical. For years my father had kept his love life hidden. Even when he was married, I rarely saw him being affectionate with his partner. With rumors of affairs with his students floating around him at every turn, he always seemed to have one foot out the door. Could he really buck a lifelong pattern?

When the semester ended, my father returned full-time to Manhattan. I continued to get an earful of his news, mostly of upcoming travel, of recent awards won. His latest book of poems, *Time & Money*, had won the National Book Critics Circle Award, and though he didn't dwell on it, I could tell he was proud of the achievement. He had been invited to Israel to read from a new translation of the book—the second English-language poet in the series after William Blake. The one poet of the pair, he quipped, still breathing.

Soon after his semester in Ann Arbor, my father initiated plans for us all to meet in Seattle in the fall. The fact that he would take the time and energy to set up such a trip said a lot. The gesture of paying a visit to his grandchildren, of including Ali and Celia in the picture, felt generous, well intentioned.

There's a photograph of my father from that trip, taken at Woodland Park Zoo in Wallingford. In it, he is clowning around with Rosie, my brother's then four-year-old girl. He has just snatched her brioche-shaped hat and stuffed it on his head. The hat's elastic band is down almost to his eyes. Along with the over-stuffed down coat, the hat makes him look especially goofy. At least Rosie thinks so. She's crouching in the corner of the shot, looking back over her shoulder at Grandpa Bill. You can almost see her thinking, *What's he doing wearing my hat?* His handsome face is screwed up, mustache standing out over his lips like a hairy comb. He's looking right at Rosie with an expression that whis-pers, *What now, little girl?* Rosie's face is lit up in utter surprise and joy.

Animated by good health, my father has been brought back to life. Gone is the self-consciousness, the intense body awareness that he usually carried around with him. Gone the old Matthews distraction he normally placed between himself and the action. He is in the thick of things: Grandpa Bill lumbering after Rosie, who is turning back to make sure she's still being chased.

People often say my father looked like Donald Sutherland. I guess there is an eerie resemblance, especially when Sutherland played the pot-smoking, student-seducing professor in *Animal House*. They both had the smoky voice, the sleepy eyes. Both were tall and slender, with narrow shoulders and long legs. In each, the sense of a vital intelligence gone slightly to seed in a wash of drink and sensualism.

Which is to say women were attracted to my father. (That he slept with his students was an open secret. I don't think he could help himself.) Drunk in their attention, he did his best to return their affection. Of course, like most men who "love women," my father was something of a womanizer. But he was also that special breed, the serial monogamist, who wanted to marry half the women he slept with. The other half he should have stayed friends with but couldn't slow the momentum.

There's a picture of my father at Bread Loaf. A pair of women's heels dangling in one hand and a drink in the other, he's wearing the beginning of a smirk, as if he's holding up primary evidence in the charge held against him and daring the viewer to say something. *Yeah, so what?* But even this is part of the put-on, some unknowable in-joke he's sharing with the person taking the photograph. Who I'd bet good money was a woman.

I often wonder what made people—friends, students, lovers— follow my father from town to town, offer to baby-sit, work around the house, drive him to readings. Why, for that matter, did his lawyer have a photo of him by her bedside—the cover of his first book, twenty-five years past—and all his books, signed "Love," on her bookshelf? Was he just another garden-variety guru? I don't think so. Here are a few lines from a poem my father wrote for, and then kept out of, his first book:

Would I like to be
every slick-crotched coed's
pin-up of a poet, Longlash
the Languid?
Sure, for a week.

He was charming, animated by what Yeats called "tragic joy." You felt good about yourself in his presence. There was something entirely genuine and easygoing about him; he could make conversation with pretty much anybody. He had the passionate intelligence of all good listeners. Part of what attracted women to my father, I imagine, was that he had the twin talents of making them laugh and listening to their stories. When he let you into his sphere, you were lifted up onto a higher plane of regard. If that meant you had to look the other way at times—to put up with his inconsistencies, lies, betrayals—then, well, so be it.

He had *sprezzatura*, as the Italians say, a certain flair in lifestyle accompanied by an air of disdain for one's own importance. On top of all that, he actually cared about other people—what they had to say, what they wrote in their poems. He was utterly without snobbery when it came to people. He could talk with anyone, would search out awkward students at the party and bring them into the conversation, playing a sort of mixed doubles with them, chasing down any ball they were too slow-footed to hit.

It was his talk, his oft admired capacity to converse—to make you laugh, to listen to you, to tell you things you didn't know—that attracted people. With a nearly photographic memory, and the audacity to pass off what he had just read as his own knowledge, my father could stitch together pieces of the night's talk into an elegant soliloquy. He was quick on his verbal feet—"witty," as almost every critic called him. With the same charisma that emanates from movie stars or politicians, he would place his attention on you. For him, I think, talk was a kind of flirtation. He hoarded a repertoire of verbal routines, which made him both awkward and exotic in a group. He had to be holding court in order to feel comfortable.

And he flirted in the manner of a shy person who has found a way to overcome fear—which is to say obsessively, as naturally as breathing—knowing what was left unsaid was more sexy than a direct statement. The glance away really an invitation. That we want to laugh even more than feel good about ourselves. That, in fact, laughing together is the first step toward intimacy. How do I know all this? That's easy. This song for my father is also the song of myself.

THAT MY FATHER often started a relationship with one woman while still with another is not a revelation. He let my mother go to be with one of his students, then left the student to be with someone else. There were so many women parading through my childhood I gave up keeping track. Some of the women were just "friends," others obviously girlfriends. Many were his students and some became our baby-sitters. All of them were attractive and smart and unnaturally interested in the two skinny boys in the living room. A few were my father's age, poets or teachers, some disappeared after a few months, others became first his "lady" friend, then his wife, then, later, his ex.

It was hard to tell what stage any of the relationships were in, or how public the connection, and I was reluctant to ask. Over the years I came up with a reliable barometer to measure the seriousness of my father's new relationship. It was simple. If the woman was tall and big-boned, like my mother, he'd leave her. If she was small-boned and short, he would stay with her until she left him. Was this his way of getting back at my mom for walking out on him when he refused to stop sleeping with other women? I don't know.

Separating

When we spurt off
in the invalid Volvo
flying its pennant of blue flames,
the neighbors group and watch.

We twist away like a released balloon.

WILLIAM MATTHEWS, "Moving"

. . . you were powerless, you were passengers . . .

MARIE HARRIS, "*Interstate*"

T HIS IS HOW I imagine it:

The student shows up at his office unexpected, with a bottle of wine in her coat pocket and an all-is-forgiven smile on her pretty mouth. What can he do?

On the drive up to the house, she gushes about her new lecture class, how brilliant the new professor is. Fine by him. He is all talked out from a long day of classes and conferences and enjoys the sound of her voice as it weaves in and out of the cold wind pouring through the windows of his old Volvo.

"I'm so glad you're finally taking me out here," she says. "I picture your sons outside shooting baskets. Willy and Sebastian, right? And you, you're up in your study in front of the typewriter. I close my eyes and I can see all that perfectly. A happy family."

He smiles sarcastically, an absentminded rebuff floating through his mind. But he keeps driving. Better to leave it alone. He thinks, instead, of his wife away with the kids. She is being unreasonable. Why can't she accept him as he is? Why does she always have to hold on to things so hard?

He slows the Volvo at Krams Corner Road to point out the two horses camped out under the shade of the willow tree, Appaloosas, brother and sister maybe. (He often does this with his sons.) Their long heads dip over the fence gracefully, buckets of feed swaying in the breeze. The horses are clearly well cared for, with acres of field stretching out behind them and a stream running across the back of the fenced property. He loves to stop to watch them.

"Just off the highway . . ." he recites, half to himself.

The student turns and smiles, knowing the James Wright poem from class. She takes up where he has left off:

". . . to Rochester, Minnesota / twilight bounds softly forth on the grass."

"And the eyes of those two Indian ponies," they recite together, laughing at their silliness, "darken with kindness."

His German shepherd, Underdog, is there to greet them at the end of the driveway, materializing from out of the lilac bush like a castle guard or a small-town cop. *Who goes there?* The dog makes him feel guilty, for he can see the dog looking around for the boys.

Quickly inside. He gives a tour of the house. She pauses to stare at the family pictures that line the hall. Placing her hands on her thin hips, she stands head tilted to the side, tongue showing between her teeth.

"She's beautiful," she says, pointing to an early portrait of his wife, the one with her pretty neck exposed and her long, thin hands laid out in front of her like a pair of porcelain gloves. "So young and pretty, but so sad."

When they get to the boys' room, she sits lightly on one of the beds, bouncing up and down to test the mattress.

"Your sons must adore you."

But he is already inspecting the trapdoor that opens to the attic, thinking that the rusty hinge might need some WD-40.

After the walk-through, she falls theatrically onto the couch and undresses one piece of clothing at a time. First her shirt in one quick tug. Then pants snaked down over her knees. Then the panties. She flings these into the air like an X-rated Mary Tyler Moore.

He watches a rain of dust shower onto her breasts.

DAD'S OUT BEHIND the house with Underdog. The student has left, bound for the Cornell inter-squad scrimmage in a tricolor taxicab. He's relieved. *Finally*, he tells himself, *the place to myself.* Marie and the kids will be back Thursday night. This gives him an extra day to straighten things up, maybe get to his work. Or maybe he'll pack his things and leave.

He's already into the second bottle of cabernet, and ideas for poetry slogans are zooming down into his head like asteroids. *There's new hope for the dead*. That's what the magazine advertisement would say: *New Hope for the Dead*. One-liners. There's the one about spiritual life, as an antidote to all the innocuous messages on church bulletin boards. This one would read: *To be warm, build an igloo*. Or how about the one on the imaginary safe-sex pamphlet handed out to poets on the eve of their first major publication? It's on premature ejaculation: *I'm sorry this poem's already finished.*

He is trying them out on the dog, his test audience, but the loyal shepherd keeps giving him the same *Aren't you coming?* look that this wandering out behind the house warrants. He tries one out on the blue jay dangling from the branch of the holly, not getting more than a few words out before the jay darts for the wire overhead.

"You good-for-nothin' jaybird."

The stereo is still on in the house, turned up high on his coveted Advent speakers. He can hear the flowing undercurrent of a jazz bass, which, by passing through the windowpanes, has taken on a silvery, humming edge. It's one of the cuts off *Kind of Blue*. He listens carefully, proud of his ear. "Flamenco Sketches," for sure.

With the sun caught behind a cloud, it all of a sudden turns cold. He's only wearing light pants, a cotton short-sleeve. Noticing how thin his arms look, he wonders when the winter will finally seep out of the spring days. It's about time for a bit of color, he thinks. About time for some warmth.

The thought of simply packing up and leaving has awakened something in him. Normally, a guilty conscience smothers the thrill. He can't (won't let himself) leave the boys. But today the feeling stands before him like an open road. *Why the fuck not?* With his book published, he can get a teaching gig just about anywhere. It's not like there's much left between them. Marie has already told him to take his women and go.

Underdog has unearthed something behind the shed. His narrow hindquarters wiggle eagerly, tail wagging, as he digs his front paws and snout into the ground. The music has stopped momentarily. My father waits for the next cut. It takes so long to come on that he thinks maybe he got the other tune wrong: that the album is now over and the needle is treading water at the center of the rotating disc. But then it comes. Like a heartbeat it comes (*dum . . . dum dum . . . dum dum . . . dum dum . . .*): its "All Blues" pulse strutting confidently, slowly forward with the inevitable momentum of the blues. His body rattling vibrantly in the day.

The sun's come out. He is past the yard now, out beyond the two old shaggy willows. It feels good to be ambulating. He can still hear the music. Miles has moved into his opening chords, as though dressing for the show, fixing his tie in the mirror. And if the rest of the band is the song's mise-en-scène, then the bass is the slanting sun, thrumming through his veins like aged Scotch.

Now Underdog has rejoined him under the trees, a wet smear of dirt on his snout. Standing at the edge of the field, hand up to his drunken hair, my father looks out at the old apple trees. He's not sure if he's going to cry, scream, or pull down armfuls of crab apples and chuck them (*Thwap!*) at the barn door like a boy (*Thwap!*) practicing to be a great pitcher. *Thwap*.

He decides to keep moving, to walk out into the woods. "Nobody here but us chickens," he tells the dog. And then a few steps later: "Nobody knows the trouble we've seen." And though with each step the pulse of the song gets fainter, he keeps heading out into the field. He knows the land, knows the song. Knows when it's time to come in, when Trane will step into the current of his solo. He's got the bass in his blood now. He knows what to do. He'll just keep walking the dog.

Visions like these keep coming to me—as snapshots, fantasies—floating around in my head as though some old photo album has been loosed and dispersed. Shots of Willy and me standing defiant in our little-boy shorts, baseball bats gripped in our hands and determined looks on our faces. A blurry picture of Willy and me out in the snow, lost in our snowsuits and gloves, Underdog's big German shepherd head at chin level.

Then there's the shot of Dad: a young man leaning tall against the Volvo, his mustache small and his face pale and youthful. And one of Mom: slender, tomboyish, beautiful in some late sixties minidress. She is pushing me on a swing. I'm looking over my shoulder at her as four-year-olds tend to do—in awe, in love. I'm saying, *Don't ever stop pushing me*. I'm saying, *Not too high*.

Now we're in Ithaca. Willy and I are at a Cornell football game with Dad in the dead of winter. Ed Marinaro is the star running back. It is so cold—freezing rain and snow—that we watch from behind the fogged-up glass of the stadium's swinging doors. We are standing in the tunnel that the players run out of at the start of the game. The action is far away; I am warm and happy, and have no need to actually follow the plays. I hang on to my father's hand and mouth the words "Ed Marinaro" over and over.

Willy and I are playing Rocket with our dad, kicking the red rubber ball high into the sycamore tree and waiting for it to ricochet off branches and down into our arms. (Two points for a clean catch, one if it bounces first.) And there I am, alone, doing my boy best to associate the slick basketball with the warped driveway rim. Running with Underdog down along a fence line, looking for Willy, who has disappeared and threatens to pop up at any moment. Wanting to get so close to him that he can't surprise me. Wanting to get as far away as I can.

There are more images. The one of my dad in his twenties. In it, he is a young poet about to publish his first book. In his squinting eyes can be read both the promise he possesses and his excited awareness of it. He's got on a leather jacket, collar upturned, and his hair is long in a late-Beatles way. I don't usually caption my memories, but this carries one. It reads: "Handsome Young Poet on the Rise."

But when I turn the picture over—labeled "Autumn 1970"—and then flip it back, I see a different story. In this one, my father is a husband to an unhappy wife who suspects he's being unfaithful and wants a trial separation.

He denies the accusation and continues to pack.

"I'm going to give a reading. I'll be back on Monday," he shouts emphatically through the doorway, balled socks clenched in his hand. "Can't you understand that?"

She stands in the kitchen, shouts up through the ceiling, "Your father is off screwing a coed."

The argument began an hour earlier when Dad mentioned his student. I am not sure, but I think he was making a joke. But Mom stopped his talking by standing stock-still, drawing her hands into tight fists, and letting out a big yell. (I knew then to go upstairs.) Now they are into a full-blown shouting match, fighting about the house, whether or not we should move from it.

"That is ridiculous," he shouts. I am sitting at the top of the stairs, just out of sight, my Converse All-Stars propped against the bathroom doorjamb, picking at the rubber and listening to every word. I can picture Dad's neck turning crimson.

"You are being absolutely ridiculous," he says. "Can you hear yourself? Can you hear yourself right now? A fucking farmhouse? No phone? That is just not feasible, Marie!"

He stands in the hall looking at Mom, who sits at the table smoking, huddled over the ashtray.

My dad has been promoted to full professor at Cornell. With the increase in salary they can afford a bigger house. That's what Mom says, anyway. She has her hopes set on a farmhouse even farther out in the country, as far away from the claustrophobic academic atmosphere as possible. She wants to move into a place with real space, with windows looking out onto a field, a dirt-road driveway of her own, and no telephone. I hear all this on our drives to and from school.

"Why can't you admit it?" she shouts back at him. "Why are you lying? Just admit it, Bill. You can't *not* fuck your students."

"We're discussing two different issues here," he says with that exasperated tone in his voice. "You must learn to separate things."

Mom stubs out her cigarette in quick little stabbing gestures.

"No," she tells him, her voice growing softer. "This is all the same damn thing."

.   .   .

THE STUDENT CALLED earlier that month. I stayed on the line to listen as Mom was told that her husband didn't love her anymore. That he was not being fulfilled in the marriage, either. Mom said over the phone, "This is not news." After the woman hung up, Mom flung the phone down on the table. I could hear her voice coming through the receiver.

"I'm only twenty-five years old," she whispered. "I'm too young to be used up."

I saw the student at one of Dad's readings. She wore cutoffs like she was going swimming, and a turtleneck sweater. She even picked me up once after school and brought me to Dad's office. I remember her peppermint soap smell, the way her smile lifted and her hands kept slipping coolly over my wrist. She let me pick the song on the car radio. I never told Mom this.

Soon after the call, Mom pulled us out of homeroom and drove straight to Grandma and Grandpa's house in Rye, New York. In Mom's mind, the marriage was over. Dad had ruined it. To get through the last highway toll, she had us search the seat cracks for loose change.

We stayed a week before Dad could convince Mom to come back. We were able to run around on the golf course behind the house, play a rough form of tennis with the neighborhood kids, six to a side, and stay up late watching television. If it had been up to me, we would never have returned home.

MOM KNOWS HER remark about doing without a phone will provoke him, but she can't help herself. She pictures the farm-house as if it is a photograph etched in her mind. She sees it from all sides, from up close and far away; sees one bare room leading through a tall doorway into the next; sees me and Willy, herself, even Dad, happy together there. Underdog at the door with a dead woodchuck in his mouth.

"I can't believe you even thought to consider that place," Dad says, returning to the kitchen. He is attempting to get on her good side. Mom picks up the ashtray and hurls it at the dining room wall. When she turns and sees me on the stairs, the expression on her face scares me. I don't know how to look back at her.

Eventually, their anger subsides. Dad goes out front to pack up the car while Mom sits out on the back porch. She won't talk to me. Dad comes over to say goodbye, but Mom won't look up or respond. I guess she doesn't see the point. Eventually he leaves, mussing up my hair before he turns away. I want to go with him, but then I don't. Mom doesn't look up even when she hears the car's tires on the gravel. If she had, she would have seen the exhaust from the tailpipe floating up like a gray balloon.

"Your father," she says into her glass of wine, "is a bastard."

My brother comes home, bustling with reckless energy. And soon he gets me going, as he always does. We talk at the same time, playing "jinx jinx-shot" and trading punches, doing everything in our power to capture Mom's attention. Then we get hungry and want Mom to draw with us. Willy pushes my head down into the couch and won't let me up until I start to cry. Mom sends Willy upstairs to his room, then calls him back to ask nicely if we could perhaps be good to our mother and spend the next hour playing quietly.

After dinner Mom reminds us that our father will be gone all weekend. We absorb the news—this kind of absence is not new—

and then walk upstairs as fast as we can without running. Mom hears us fighting in our room, but doesn't have it in her to come and break it up. When she tucks us in, I can't help asking if Dad will come home soon. Later, I hear my mother crying softly to herself in the tub while the bathwater goes cold.

I AM IN the kitchen with Mom when she makes the call. Willy's out somewhere with Underdog.

"Jan? It's Marie. Would you like to ride out with me to see the house? The farmhouse. Yes, today. Out past Johnson's dairy. I've called the man and he says he can show it this afternoon. No, I don't have it. Bill and I had a fight. He drove off. I know, I know. I let him. He's out of town for the weekend. Buffalo. Yup. What else? Oh, let's not talk about it. It depresses me."

But Jan can't come—she doesn't have a sitter—and we are left to find our own way out to the farm. Mom lets me call Mr. Kendrick, who says he will send his sons right over with the automobile. That's the word he uses, "automobile."

"Keep it all weekend," he says. "We have no need of it right now."

"That's okay," I say. Mom is mouthing a response, moving her hands as though we were playing charades. "We just need it for the afternoon. My mom will call up this evening when we return. Thank you, Mr. Kendrick."

The Kendrick brothers arrive ten minutes later, leaving

together in their father's truck. No one says much of anything. Mom just hands them jars of jam and thanks them for their trouble. They seem in a hurry to leave.

The old man stands by the big blue mailbox like he said he would, a bullet-gray International Harvester truck parked behind him. He waves his hand once to catch Mom's eye. "He's out of a Frost poem," she says to herself. He has a shock of white hair, and he stands straight when he looks into the sun. I can picture him splitting wood, leaning over to right the tipped log.

He says "Hello" in a clipped voice, harsher than I imagined it. "You must be the lady who called about seeing the old farm."

"I am. This is my son, Sebastian. My husband and I are excited to look at the place. It sounds like just what we're looking for."

I keep my mouth shut.

"Your husband ought to see the place first before you run ahead and make a decision," the old man says. "It's not in the best of shape, I told you that over the phone. Needs work. Wintering, mostly. Maybe some paint. My boys'll help you with that, if you'd like. It's no palace, mind you, just an old farm going to seed."

We can't see the house from the road, and I wonder if we are going to have to drive. I want a ride in the old man's truck.

"It's just over the hill," the old man says. "We can walk if you care to."

Hugging herself, my mom replies, "That's fine." She should have brought her coat.

The late afternoon sun drops into the pine forest in a way that makes me think a giant lake lies at the end of the driveway. Maybe it is the spaces between the trees, but I can't help imagining a shimmering body of water ahead.

I watch Mom try to keep her attention on the old man's idle talk, but I can see her mind wandering ahead. She is a girl again, catching up with her friends who are singing out silly songs and holding hands. They are heading for the beach and will spend the whole day there. The gravel road is hard on her bare feet. She whispers to herself, "It doesn't hurt, it doesn't hurt, it doesn't hurt" until she reaches the tar.

"In the heart of winter you won't make it down this road," the old man is saying. "It's best to park at the mailbox and walk in. It takes getting used to, but over time you'll come to appreciate the walk through the trees. My sons used to complain about it, but now that's what they talk about when they work on the place. They tell me about the walk in. It's funny."

Mom tunes in near the end, only half aware he has mentioned walking in the snow.

"What about groceries?"

We have come to the top of the hill and are looking down into a deeply shaded gully. The trees give way to a field of high grass running ragged down a slope. The road cuts along the borderline between forest and field, eventually leading to a small farm at the meadow's southeast corner. A wedge of sun drops down onto the old farmhouse and barn, bathing the buildings in a golden light.

"Groceries?" The man seems perplexed. I know what she means.

"In winter. Snow . . ." she says.

"A sled," I say.

The man looks at me for the first time. His face is stern, and I see that he knows how to get angry. I have to look away.

"That's right, young man, you take them in on a sled."

Mom has taken out her checkbook. The farm stands in front of her, a photograph of life the way she wants to live it. The beach dunes shift about in her memory. She has no use for a sled.

"I'm not sure what you were expecting, Mrs. Matthews."

"It's beautiful," she says. And as she says it, the words "big house, little house, backhouse, barn" come into her mind. She pictures herself jumping rope with her friends, calling out the song. "It's everything I've ever wanted."

"That may be," the old man says, hand to his eyes.

"How much?" I hear her saying. Her voice is different. She sounds like some rich widow. "How much would you need for an initial down payment, I mean? To hold it until my husband returns?"

"Oh, I imagine a thousand dollars would do."

The old man seems to be surveying the land, taking stock of what he sees. If I were older, I would ask him why he is selling off his property. He might have grown up here.

But Mom carefully rips out the check and hands it to the man. He folds the paper twice, slipping it into his shirt pocket. When she goes to write the figure into her check record, there is a zero balance. She knows this. It hasn't occurred to her to care.

❧

HE PULLS THE blinds together, shutting out the emptiness of the parking lot. He is dead tired. The reading was a success. The last poem went particularly well, its rhythm expressed exactly—his voice, always an asset, left to its work. And when he came to the end of the reading, to the crescendo of the long poem, it felt distinctly as though he were pulling together a tapestry of insight and deep emotion. He was a magician waving his cloak and disappearing. Sneaking outside for a smoke before the applause had even died down.

After the reading, some of the professors and their students had insisted on taking him out for a drink. They spent an hour standing around a noisy sports bar shouting at each other over the music. A basketball game flickered on the television. The group argued over whether creative writing could truly be taught in academia, though the whole question bored him. It was a matter of teaching preparedness. He wanted only to get back to the motel, to call Marie and somehow make up for the fight. But there seemed no polite way out.

At a certain point, he turned his attention to the game. One of the professors had launched into a lengthy diatribe on postmodern narrative, which he aimed at two bored and hapless graduate students. One of the students, to his credit, came to the defense of good, old-fashioned storytelling, but the professor kept interrupting.

Luckily, there was a basketball game to hide in. A third student—an angelic young woman whose straight blond hair reminded him of Candice Bergen in *Carnal Knowledge*—turned to the game as well, confessing that she knew next to nothing about the sport. The Celtics were playing the Lakers in a mid-season game. There was a play-off atmosphere, as the announcers liked to say. Bill Russell was a whirling dervish out on the floor, grabbing rebounds and sending outlet passes downcourt to a cherry-picking Don Nelson; in answer, Jerry West was draining long-range jumpers from all over the court.

"What's the point?" she said in his ear, smelling of her borrowed perfume, of sweat and cigarette smoke. "Of watching ten large men with thyroid conditions sweat as they run down the court and stuff an orange ball into a basket? Can you explain it to me?"

He knew the young woman was only flirting with him, doing her best to engage him in some kind of dialogue. But he didn't know what to say. How do you explain your faith to a nonbeliever?

Outside the bar, she leaned into him, arms around his neck. They kissed. Drawing back, he felt the cold air sweep across his brow. Her young breasts pushed into his chest. He thought to himself, *I have no idea.* He said it again, this time out loud. He repeated the phrase once more, under his breath, easing into the low-slung car.

"I loved your poems," she had said. "Especially the last one."

She'd wanted to hear him read it to her. They were parked outside his motel. He recited something Wordsworthian (". . . after many wanderings, many years"), pretending he had come up with it that night in the bar. Then he kissed her. He knew he shouldn't, but he couldn't come up with a convincing enough argument to stop the momentum. She kissed back.

AS HE OPENS the hot-water faucet, he wonders why he stopped, why he stepped out of the car, apologized to the young woman. He had done this through the rolled-down window. She seemed perplexed at first, then disappointed, then amused. They talked for a while, the door a barrier between them, her face exposed by the parking lot lights. Then she was gone, and he went off to piss in the bushes, realizing as he swayed beside a tree just how drunk he really was.

Lying in the steam and near-scalding water, the beginnings of a migraine settling into his skull, he thinks again to call Marie. It is well past one, but he is pretty sure she'll be up. He imagines the house dark except for the downstairs hall light. Underdog sighing on the wool rug under the stairs. The boys asleep upstairs or at a friend's house. Marie is in the kitchen, rinsing out old paintbrushes for something to do. The radio is on. The news or maybe some jazz. The phone will ring and ring. She will look up but not reach for the receiver.

I DON'T REMEMBER how we end up outside, or where she gets a glass of wine. (Maybe I fell asleep.) But we are in the backyard now, a few feet from the clothesline. Mom is on her own, her husband out sleeping with some woman. She decides to leave him. The idea sits on her tongue like a swallow of wine. "Damn it all," she says half to me, half to herself. "I'm drunk."

The moon is a sliver behind the trees. The branches of the pear tree need pruning; the fruit lies scattered like discharged gun shells. Mom looks up at the sky. She is swaying on her feet. I can almost feel the wind pushing its way through her shirt, lifting it up ever so slightly and laying it down lightly against the bare skin of her chest.

She's talking to herself now. "I'm tired of being a second-rate wife, a second-best lover, Mrs. Professor, Mrs. Poet's Wife, cook, cleaner, chauffeur. I will not be in competition with every female grad student who gets a crush on my husband. They can have him. He certainly seems to prefer them."

And: "We'll head east. All the way to the ocean. You boys can sleep out in the trees and fields and climb mossy rocks all day. I'll get a job."

This idea seems to calm her, loosening her whole body. I think this is a good idea. I always feel happy on the beach—the roar of surf engulfing me, the wind whipping around.

When Mom goes over to the herb garden, I follow her. I am afraid she'll fall down. "This I will miss," she says. "But that's all." She pulls off a few mint leaves, crushing them with her fingers, and then drops them into her wine. She is a good mom; I wish we'd go inside.

She makes her way farther back into the yard instead, coming to a halt at the dried-up grapevine. I follow behind her like a shadow. She laughs out loud when she spots the compost pile with its falling-over cylinder of wire. It has dried up ages ago, even the insects have left it alone.

"That's perfect," she says. "Just perfect."

She wants her dress to rip on the wire, wants to run the palm of her hand over it and tattoo her pain there. Instead, she pushes the loose flap aside and sits down on the pile. It's soft like a sand dune. Her wine is almost done. There is more but the house is far away, lit up like an ocean liner.

"We'll stay the night," she tells me, taking me into her arms. "Sleep here until the morning comes. Then we'll go fetch Willy. We can be ready and packed within the hour."

"What about Underdog?"

"He can stay with your father."

Back & Forth

remember: you
are simply another
change-of-address

MARIE HARRIS, "*Interstate*"

If I lived with my sons
all year I'd be less sentimental
about them

WILLIAM MATTHEWS, "Moving Again"

PEOPLE ASK ME where I grew up. I don't know how to answer. I say, "I moved a lot."

Or: "My parents divorced when I was little; I moved back and forth between them."

Sometimes, if there's an atlas handy, or a map of the United States hanging on a wall, I'll trace the route for them. I start down in Chapel Hill, North Carolina, my birthplace, then move my finger quickly to upstate New York, first to Aurora, then to Ithaca. This is the precise route, I say, of my dad's early professional life.

If they push me, I'll give the chronology. My parents divorced when I was five, I'll say. By ten, I had already attended three schools in three towns in two states. By fifteen, I had gone to four more schools in two new towns, one city, three states. Willy and I lived with my mom for the first four years after the split. We'd stay with our father summers and visit during any school vacation for which he could afford the transportation.

The army brats in the crowd nod their heads. They know first-hand the emotional calculus that lies behind this simple arithmetic. Others, unschooled in such matters, ask: "Wasn't it hard to move that much?" I can only shrug my shoulders and bring them back to the map. My parents' divorce has become the X that declares "You Are Here." From this point on, I must use both hands: pointing fingers cast out in opposite directions.

When the marriage fell apart, my mother gathered us up and fled. We landed in Portsmouth, New Hampshire, because she had a sister there, because she missed living by the ocean. Looking for a place to anchor, she escaped an old life by traveling out to find a new one. Dad followed her east so he could be near us, landing a temporary teaching position at Emerson College in Boston. He rented a house halfway between, in Andover, and had us down on the weekends. When the job at the University of Colorado was offered for the next year, he couldn't turn it down. He packed up his Volvo one more time and drove out west:

> *The dust of not sleeping*
> *drifts in my mouth, and five or six*
> *miles slur by uncounted.*
> *I say I hate long distance*
> *drives but I love them.*
>
> ("Iowa City to Boulder")

We flew out to see him for Christmas, crowding into his ratty rental in the university district. He drove us up to the mountains the last day, in the middle of a snowstorm, and we got out at a switchback and spent an hour climbing around a rocky riverbed.

"So what do you call 'home'?" a few brave souls ask.

A good question. By way of answer, I tell a story about life after the divorce—a story that both parents have claimed as their own. In it, we have just moved into a new apartment complex; bags are piled in the hall. Our phone isn't hooked up yet, and the place smells of ammonia and Murphy's Oil Soap. One of the boys—let's say it was me—runs to the window and looks eagerly outside. Bare trees clump behind the parking lot, a rusty swing set idles on a patch of dead grass. Willy joins me at the window. In both versions of the story, I turn back and ask: "Where are the friends?"

Here's what I want to say but never can: that when you move back and forth between your parents, you become a spy. Schooled in the art of confidence, you learn to slip on the appropriate mask. Your parents do not ask you to be this way. If they are well meaning—as were mine—they do not wish this condition upon you. But it happens anyway. Any divorce is a battle; all separation a matter of strategy, retreat and attack, compromise and trickery. The children become the messengers, adept at picking their way through emotional land mines. They become the keeper of secrets, passing across the field of battle bearing a white flag and a scroll.

More than anything else, what a child of divorce learns is that things change. People come into your life and leave. Strangers become your family, and sometimes your family can turn into strangers or simply disappear. You learn this early; it becomes a part of your metabolism. You pick up the faint goodbye in each hello. You are always looking for the betraying fingers behind the back.

All this is true. But so is this: Willy and I looked at each new place, each new move, not so much as a leaving behind, or a fragmentation, as an arrival, an accretion. We were game. We were back-and-forthers.

Willy AND I bivouacked that first year in the Sagamore Apartments, a working-class complex teeming with kids who soon taught us all the choice hideouts and graveyard meeting spots. We attended a progressive elementary school, only a short bike ride into the center of Portsmouth. We loved our teachers, made friends easily. Mom made friends, too, with some of the teachers at our school, and began meeting artists at the readings and openings typical of such a small, artsy tourist town. She hooked up with a group of summer-stock actors, a mix of local performers and Equity players up from New York for the Prescott Park Arts Festival, who gathered for drinks at the Press Room. Slowly, she let herself relax into her new life.

At some point in that first year of possibility, my mom met a painter at a gallery opening. Arthur charmed her with his interest in her poetry, with his stories of bohemian life in the country. She was impressed by the image of a big, unruly garden and endless, rolling fields. They dated for a few months. He painted her portrait. Then, on one of the first true days of summer, we packed our things into the dilapidated station wagon and drove inland an hour, over Parker Mountain into the slowly disappearing forests of central New Hampshire.

In comparison to Portsmouth, with its cobblestone streets and lively scene of cafés, with its bars and used-clothes boutiques, the downtown "square" of Center Barnstead, New Hampshire, was disappointing. There was nothing there but a small gathering of run-down houses, a two-room library, a fire/police station, a general store with a rusted-out Mountain Dew sign out front, a church, a two-pump gas station, and, just west of the small river bridge, a seasonal real estate office and the local Elks chapter. I wanted Mom to turn the car around and head back to the ocean.

We lived at the end of a dirt road in the middle of nowhere. Arthur's house had long, slanted halls, high ceilings, and a huge painting studio in the back that smelled perpetually of turpentine and cigarettes. In its own funky way, the place was a farm. The property was packed with animals. We even had a cantankerous goat, Skull Murphy, named after a popular professional wrestler. At various times, we looked after pigs, chickens, geese, and, if my memory serves me, guinea hens and exotic ducks with names like Indian Runner. Not to say we lived a farming life. Far from it.

Arthur raised terriers—miniature bulls and Borders, mostly. He admired them for their tenacity. He was particularly fond of Adelaide, a fearless Border terrier who followed woodchucks down holes and attacked them face-on. He often said he liked my mom because she was "game," which was Arthur-speak for independent. I think he also wanted a live-in model. In the long run, I don't think he was much different from my dad, talking a good liberated game but still balking at doing his share of the chores.

Arthur was a Boston Jew happily out of place in rural New Hampshire painting away his afternoons. But he liked kids and allowed us the run of the place. He was a temperamental man who swung back and forth between bouts of ranting and sulking. His moods passionate and showy but never fueled by anger, Arthur showered most of his love on his dogs and funneled his anger into his watercolors. He was big and hairy, soft-faced with a scruffy black beard and expressive with his hands, all of which made him the perfect harmless monster: he'd yell "Goyim!" at us or shoo us out of the house like we were geese. We would laugh and run away.

When money got tight, which it often did, Mom would mix goat's milk with powdered milk and pour it in an old store-bought container for appearances. (We knew with one whiff!) When things became really tight, she bartered one of Arthur's paintings. Once she landed a woodstove in exchange, another time she paid a particularly overdue gas credit card bill by convincing the guy at Mobil that he needed something to "brighten up" the office. Other things we got by bartering Arthur's paintings: tax preparation services, two used cars, dental services for Arthur, and a miniature bull terrier named Maude.

Cooped up in his painting studio for hours, Arthur would only come out to feed the dogs or take a piss. We did our best to avoid him and went to find Mom, who would be either in her herb garden, in her study working on a poem, or out in the henhouse collecting eggs. Once in a while, Arthur's artist friends would come in from Boston, and there'd be a big party. I remember this man who, I was convinced, with his smooth black skin and close-cropped Afro, had to be the Celtics shooting guard, Jo Jo White. The whole night I followed him around in awe, too nervous to ask for his autograph. Later, I found out he wasn't the guy.

WHEN WE VISITED my father in Colorado those first summers, he was living with Sharon, a former student from his Cornell poetry workshop, who had been his off-and-on girlfriend ever since. She was there in Andover, too, but it wasn't until our time together in Boulder that I started to become aware of her quiet presence. Sharon was small. She had straight dirty-blond hair that she wore cut in a stark bob. She was thin, small-boned, and her skin was pale even at the height of a Colorado summer. Her blue eyes were her most startling feature: they brimmed over with good nature. They shone out in playful spirit, broadcasting her seemingly boundless energy for life.

But she was no waif. Sharon was most happy *doing* things—cooking a meal, driving to an event, piecing together a puzzle. She wore muted cotton clothing in a variety of pastel colors, walked in soft-soled shoes, and lugged around a purse everywhere she went. She loved cats, listened to music avidly, loved to talk. And when she laughed, her mirth burst out of her as part "Ha!" and part gleeful chuckle. It made me want to find ways to amuse her.

When she was upset—which, living with my father, was often—she wore a clown's frustration on her face: the light in her eyes would shut down, her brow would drop, and her lips would form a narrow line. When really peeved, she'd clench her fists and sigh. Sharon came from Utah, and as a kid I always wondered if that was where she got her enthusiasm—for it seemed to me then a kind of quintessential western openness and friendliness. Her whole family had it. Or maybe it was just who she was. I didn't know. All I knew was Willy and I couldn't always deal with it. She was almost *too* open. Too friendly. We were used to East Coast bohemians, veterans at fielding the spins and twists of their sophisticated banter.

But I warmed up to Sharon. I liked driving down the mountain with her on errands. It was like we were heading out on a journey—just me and her. Like being back together with Mom, too, but also a little like having a girlfriend. I was happy in her company, nervous, almost giddy. I couldn't name the feeling. It wasn't about being caught: we weren't doing anything wrong. It was more a too-muchness feeling. I just wanted the ride to keep going.

Our house was ranch style and situated far up on Jamestown Star Route, a switchbacking road overlooking Boulder. Willy and I had rooms in the basement, which meant the walls were cement and spiders oozed into our rooms between the cracks. There was a sliding glass door leading out to our backyard; a runway of scrub and rock and cactus down into pine forest. Underdog would wake me in the middle of the night by sticking his wet snout on my arm, and I'd climb out of bed and let him outside. Sometime before morning he'd scratch on the door to be let back in.

As an antidote to the daily afternoon lull, Willy and I made up elaborate games to test our hand-to-eye coordination and our courage, like throwing pebbles into the tiny hole in the garage door or riding our bikes down the massively steep hill with no hands and then speed-walking them back up again. When we had nothing better to do, we went looking for Underdog in among the ponderosa pines, invariably finding him deep inside its branches, happily camped in the shade. Dad's room was upstairs, off the dining room. We'd spend a good deal of our time bouncing on that big bed. Or we'd congregate in the living room to listen to records and make elaborate drawings.

I was listening to Elton John a lot back then. His *Greatest Hits* had just come out. "Your Song" was my favorite. I'd play it over and over on my new hi-fi. Something about those lyrics got me, especially the line "How wonderful life is when you're in the world." It made me miss my mom, hope my dad would never die, that I would never die, or grow up, and that Sharon would stay around. All at once.

IN NEW HAMPSHIRE, Mom took us to a lot of movies. Once a week, we'd pile into Arthur's busted-up station wagon and drive the fifteen miles to neighboring Pittsfield. *Jeremiah Johnson. Fantastic Voyage. Grizzly Adams. Old Yeller. It's a Mad, Mad, Mad, Mad World.* We didn't care what was playing so long as we were getting out of Barnstead for a while.

On any particular Saturday afternoon a packed house of restless kids from the surrounding towns swarmed the place. Accompanied by parents or left unattended, they ruled the theater. Boys ran in packs of six or eight, commandeered entire rows, spending most of the movie talking, fighting, or throwing popcorn. An ever-growing gaggle of girls sat in the middle of the theater, on both sides of the aisle, buzzing and bubbling. It seemed everybody in the place talked back at the movie and, if a nerve was hit, to each other. They would stand up in the projector's dusty beam to shout some inane remark into the darkness. Then they told each other to "shut up!" or "fuck off!" Fourteen-year-olds belted out swearwords just to hear their own voices, which caused their buddies to break up in laughter or, worse, follow suit.

The Pittsfield Theater—the whole town for that matter—was long past run-down, having moved through dilapidation over the years and slipped into decrepitude. The popcorn machine, the curtain rig, the projector, and the entrance turnstile were all in various states of disrepair. Drafts ran through the building like currents of springwater in a pond. The lady at the counter took our money without comment and made change from a rusted metal box.

I both loved and dreaded going to movies there. Pittsfield was a tough town and the kids, for the most part, were older or not from my elementary school. I would roam a bit and get caught up in the room's electricity, but when the lights went down and the ineffective "hush's" and "shhhh's" went up with the curtain, I was happy to be blanketed in dark. I didn't have to participate in the bedlam. My world shrank to the size of the screen; the only thing left of the outside world the pressure of my mom's arm next to mine.

Once, in the middle of the movie *Sounder*, after an hour of unrelenting verbal assault at the screen, my mom turned around and shouted for everyone to sit down, shut up, and stop yelling racist remarks at the black man on-screen. "You should be ashamed of yourselves," she said to the stunned crowd.

I was both awed by my mother's outburst and scared of what might happen in response. I waited for the inevitable hailstorm of abuse to pour down upon her—and, by extension, me—sure we'd be banished from the theater, walked out by phantom ushers to a chorus of jeers. But no one said anything. The place was eerily quiet, the only sound the crunching of hunters' footsteps in the celluloid forest. More amazing still: no one said anything for the rest of the film. For probably the first and last time, that audience sat and watched the movie in silence. And, I like to think now, they really *felt* that movie's message, were acutely aware of how unjustly that black man had been treated—not only by the characters in the movie but by themselves. When I walked out of that theater, I was proud. I was with *her*.

·   ·   ·

houlder. We have bangs down to our eyes and blond hair hanging ow over our ears. My jeans are held up by a leather belt with a arge metal buckle. We smile at the person taking the photo (Dad? Sharon? One of his other girlfriends?). But Willy's is not really a mile, more of a mock-menacing growl, as if he was only pretending he wanted to push me into the fence but secretly wanted to.

Looking at that photo now, I can't help wondering what was oing through my brother's mind during those years right after the ivorce. Was he aware of his dominance over me? That he was oth my tormentor and my hero? Or was he, too, feeling pushed nto a fence, caught between the interlocked wills of two warring arents? I wonder if he felt unseen, that no one seemed to notice hat he was hurt and afraid. That he'd just been left there, left to ke care of his idiot brother. So he starts pushing back. He'll yell they don't hear him—yell louder than they do!—and kick if ey don't remember he's there. He'll take it out on his younger rother, all this rage and confusion and sorrow.

(The young father taking the picture sees everything but oesn't know what to do. Maybe he feels the youngest son needs to oughen up, must learn to withstand his older brother's wrath. Maybe he doesn't want to become authoritarian, like his own ther. Maybe the duties of fatherhood scare him.)

"Get out of here, get out of my way!" Willy hisses under his eath. And, at the same time, in a whisper, he implores: "Stay re. Don't leave me."

CORDING TO THE custody arrangements, after seven years th my mother, we were to go live with my father. For years, Dad d been pushing to be the primary parent, adamant that it wasn't

MY FATHER LOVED to cook dinner for us. I think cooking was the easiest, least complicated way for him to be a parent. (That, and playing sports.) He'd put on his Kliban apron, the one with the cat wearing a big chef's hat, set out all the meal's ingredients, and oil the pans. We'd often join him in the kitchen, eager to complete some small task. Chopping parsley, husking corn. Mostly, we'd watch. The way he diced onions, leaning over at the waist, all focus in his arms and hands, rocking the knife over the wooden block. The way he seemed to dance between the stove and the counter, singing snatches of the song blasting from the stereo. The little flourish he'd give in his wrist and fingers when he finished something that took concentration—a flip of steaks in the pan, separating an egg white.

Dad took us to movies, too. Maybe he was trying to make up for all the years he spent as a vacation parent. We went to see the Marx Brothers, samurai films, foreign flicks, old westerns, and the latest James Bond. I remember walking out of Woody Allen's *Sleeper* into the day's glare and being caught up in the movie's zaniness: the huge vegetables, the disembodied nose, the rubber suit skidding across the lake like a catcher's mitt gone berserk. That wild Dixieland sound track. Holding my dad's hand and dancing off energy. And I remember the ride home up the backtracking mountain road into Left Hand Canyon, Willy leaning over the front seat, retelling the best parts of the movie until they were no longer funny.

We went to all of Woody Allen's films after that. I especially liked the ones that starred the kid version of Allen. With his carrot-red hair and thick glasses, and that bemused smirk he reserved for the more stupid among us, that kid had all the confidence in the world. I wanted to *be* Woody Allen. But what I had wanted more, I realize now, was to be a part of his family: to have more relatives than I could count living in my house; to have parents who argued but loved each other; and to have sisters who danced in the living room and a mother who sent me off to school with a litany of warnings and pinches. It was not my life, and it looked good.

For my twelfth birthday, my father bought me a Woody Allen record, *The Nightclub Years*. I spent hours listening to it in my room. I see now that most of the jokes were over my head. Not being Jewish, or from New York, I was often in the dark. But it didn't matter. There was enough humor in Allen's delivery—the strange clucks and clicks he made with his tongue, the abundance of surreal imagery—to make any kid's head spin.

My favorite routine on the LP was called "The Moose." It took a while, but, eventually I was able to say it straight through without mistakes. Of course, I didn't have Allen's timing and flair for the ironic, so when I recited it at my father's parties, I'm sure I butchered the nuances. But they all laughed anyway, I guess because I was just a kid—a goy at that—reciting Woody Allen. I can still remember the opening lines: "I shot a moose. I was hunting upstate New York and I shot a moose."

It was always a big deal when my father came outside to join us for a few games of "21" or when he challenged us to a round of H.O.R.S.E. He wouldn't hold back (or at least it felt that way then), giving us all we could handle from his big basketball body. We had heard his stories of high school games in Cincinnati and knew he played intramural games through the university, but we couldn't really picture our dad playing with anybody but us. He

had an archaic hook shot that he drew up from his launched by his head. It was an old Celtic hook sh Cowens than Russell—that he'd start on the baseline almost under the basket, slowly whirling into the lane extending just past our reach. He was adept at the bank and could easily drop it off the board, no matter how har from his shoulders. The only way I could score was to the corner and hoist up desperate three-pointers.

Once, in our low-ceilinged garage playing Ping-Pong hit his head on an overhanging fluorescent light. He leaning in for a slam, caught in a battle of wills with Wi for the final game and that night's mastery of the tabl inadvertently knocked himself, temple first, into the sh the light. He dropped to the ground like a sack of flour. just stood there as our dad curled in on himself. We what to do or say, feeling as each second ticked off mo guilty. It was as if by witnessing his pain we had caused

He got up eventually, slow and angry as a bear, ar paddle at the back wall. I remember one of us askir was okay.

"Of course I'm not fucking okay!" he yelled, tak body with him, leaving us there, facing each other.

THERE'S A SNAPSHOT of Willy and me from Dad. I can't be more than twelve years old. I've got my skinny arms are tan, as are Willy's under his gree striped T-shirt. In the picture I am leaning forward aga link fence. Willy stands close behind me, his big han

fair (antifeminist, in fact) that Willy and I should live only with her. And when Mom left Arthur, tired and broke and no longer in love, she finally gave in to his demands. And so three years early—in 1976, the summer after my fifth grade—my mother asked my father to take us in. He eagerly agreed.

It was horrible timing. My best friend, Alan, and I were stars on the school soccer team. I had a new girlfriend, got along with my teachers, loved wandering the woods out behind our house and taking care of the animals on the property. I had even become fond of Arthur. I wanted to put on a game face for my mother, but I was devastated. To make things worse, instead of reuniting us with our summer friends in Boulder, my father took us with him to Iowa City, where he had been offered a one-year position on the faculty of the University of Iowa's esteemed Writers' Workshop. (And he left Underdog with one of his University of Colorado students!)

Sharon had helped my father secure his position at Iowa; she had found them a small farmhouse to share, but now two kids were in the picture and she had to find a larger house to fit us all. After only a few weeks, she moved into her own place. No one explained why; she just packed her things and left. I learned years later that Dad was having a very public affair with one of the graduate students in the program. All I knew at the time: I was in a new school, without friends. I would ride my bike over to Sharon's apartment and ring her doorbell, hoping she was home. *Are you my mother?*

What I remember about that first year with Dad is being constantly cold and lonely. A brutally cold winter full of snowdrifts, cold feet, underheated rooms. I remember my father being gone a lot and Willy off with friends or at basketball practice. Even my first day at school went awry. Dad wouldn't give me a ride, saying I should walk, so I got lost in the dozen or so blocks to Longfellow Elementary. As if in a nightmare, I arrived late and had to be led to homeroom in tears. Class was, of course, already in session, and when I walked in all the students, together since first grade, stopped what they were doing and stared at me. The teacher directed me to sit in the only empty seat, smack-dab in the middle of the girls. The boys across the way snickered. The new kid had arrived, and he was a wuss. I don't think I made a friend until after Christmas.

After that miserable year in Iowa City, we moved back to Boulder. Not surprisingly, Sharon didn't return with us. She went to New York City straight from Iowa to work for the summer, then took a one-year job at Marlboro College in Vermont. I remember her joining us in Colorado the next Christmas, and my father visiting her once in the spring. There was talk of them getting married, but Dad was resistant. Sharon found out that he was having an affair with another of his students. Months later, thinking it belonged to the other woman, Dad threw out all of Sharon's stuff she'd been storing in our garage.

Willy and I were like any pair of brothers—easily bored, quick to quarrel. Willy, who had just entered ninth grade, went to one of the big high schools. I was in seventh, trapped in the limbo of middle school. We fought constantly, played Ping-Pong like madmen, stole Marlboros from my father's current carton and smoked them out behind the garage. We climbed up on the roof and threw pinecones at passing cars. We talked with our friends on the phone for hours at a time and, when Dad was busy cooking dinner, shot baskets past dark.

Willy was playing on the junior varsity soccer and basketball teams. He was also beginning to get in trouble. He and his friends would go out drinking and smoking pot, looking for something to vandalize. They skateboarded everywhere, played pinball at Midnight Silver. I wanted to come along, but Willy's friends didn't want me around. The eighteen-month age difference between us never seemed greater.

As an alternative, I made friends with a classmate who lived up the road from us, and started spending a lot of my time over at his house. I'd become too shy to have a girlfriend, but I had a Top Ten list of crushes that I would obsessively revise depending on our encounters in the halls. I was a skinny thirteen-year-old, at the beginning of a growth spurt, and recently fitted with braces. I read books constantly, rode my new ten-speed everywhere, and listened to rock-and-roll records in my room.

During that last year up in the mountains, students flowed in and out of our house as if attending a weekend party: there always seemed to be an epic, goofy game of basketball going on, and a succession of cooks working on an assembly line of stews and soups. I had a mad crush on one of my dad's students, Linda—I thought she looked like Linda Ronstadt—who took me out to movies and afterward bought me fast food at one of the taco stands on Arapaho and talked passionately about my father. There was Jorge, a hippie who brought us homemade bread once a week that was so hard, so inedible, we hid it in the bottom of the trash can after he left. And big, friendly Chris, who read us chapters from *The Hobbit* in a cast of voices. And though we didn't talk about it, Willy and I couldn't help noticing Linda coming out of my father's bedroom late at night. One morning she even appeared looking sheepish at the breakfast table.

I have one memory that serves as an emblem for those years in Colorado with my father. More accurately, it's a collage of taped-together memories. In it, I am perpetually staying up late with Dad. Some of his students are over. We're in our house, way up in Left Hand Canyon. Bob Dylan's "On a Night Like This" is playing on the stereo and bottles of wine litter the table. A fire's in the fireplace, maybe even snow outside, Dylan is crooning, and there I am, reaching some kind of kid bliss, awash in the grown-up talk and the mercury sound of the Band and Dylan's harmonica. Seven thousand feet above the sea, I'd remind myself, and the night as long and as deep as the ocean.

Change of Address

At a deepening
of the Isinglass River
I lie down in stones and tea-colored water.
I think: be careful. Do not say
home. The bones
of that word mend slowly.

MARIE HARRIS, *"Interstate"*

Sebastian cries in his sleep,
I bring him into my bed,
talk to him, rub his back.
To help his sons live easily
among the dead is a father's great work.

WILLIAM MATTHEWS, "Living Among the Dead"

SENDING WILLY AND me to live with our father might have been the hardest thing my mom ever had to do, or has had to live with. Up until that point, she had always defined herself through others: first by her role in her family, the oldest of ten; then by the man in her life; later, as mother to her children. After four years on her own with two boys, after long winters of struggling to get by, she needed to reconnect with that nineteen-year-old girl inside her—needed to find a passion for life again. Just once, she was going to be out on her own, free to figure it all out.

After she left Arthur, Mom moved in with her sister Cathy, in a three-room apartment over Emilio's Deli in downtown Portsmouth. For a while, she worked as a ticket taker at the local playhouse, wrote ad copy, used her melodious voice to record radio voice-overs. It was a somewhat lonely life but an independent one. She wrote new poems, dated men here and there. She missed her boys terribly, wanting to have us for more than a few months each year. She worried constantly about leaving us with our father, willing herself to believe that we might thrive in his primary care. And worried that we'd feel she abandoned us, that we wouldn't forgive her for leaving.

My mother had traveled a long way from her debutante ball in Rye, New York, and her two years of college at Georgetown. She had made it through sweltering days in Chapel Hill, pregnant and with a one-year old at her side; cooked and cleaned and took care of the kids and hosted an endless number of my father's faculty parties. As a young faculty wife, she was simply following her husband from job to job. She got to her own work when she could and struggled to finish college on the side. She wanted to experience more, be more. Fight less, laugh more.

Like many women of her generation, my mother moved from being a teenager to being a mom with no in-between. She had been in love with her husband but finally couldn't accept his infidelities. When her marriage started to crumble, she both wanted a divorce and was afraid of being on her own. She was disappointing her parents, she knew, but had grown tired of fighting against a Catholic upbringing in conflict with her recently raised consciousness. She had been brought up to believe she could do anything, go anywhere, achieve whatever she wanted, and so couldn't reconcile that birth control was not permitted by the church and that women were treated as second-class citizens at every level.

It was 1976, and the women's movement had been picking up speed, empowering women like my mother to start talking about the things they'd been putting up with for years. Marie Matthews was Marie Harris again. She was thirty years old. Her first book of poems, *Raw Honey*, had come out from Alice James Books, a feminist cooperative in Boston, and she was driving into the city once a week from Portsmouth to put in her share of co-op work, ecstatic to be surrounded by such dynamic, committed women.

Arthur's portraits of Mom—some oil, others watercolor—were hanging up in her new apartment. Whenever I'd visit, I'd stare at them, remembering hungrily our time in Barnstead. How Arthur would pose Mom in a big rocking chair in the corner of his drafty studio, and she'd curl up in a blanket with a book and her tea. And how he'd paint three or four watercolors in rapid succession, break for a smoke, then go back at it. Willy and I would sneak around the back of the house, braving the killer goose that roamed the yard for a quick peek through the sliding glass door.

In one of the portraits, she is in a rocking chair reading a book. Her head is tilted down. She seems sad. It's as if Arthur had unwittingly captured her restless spirit, contained momentarily in the wave-current of rocking. She is biding her time until something new comes along, pinned against her backdrop like a butterfly.

Despite being broke and estranged from her sons, there was a lot for Mom to be happy about. For the first time she had her own identity as a poet. She was working on a second book, *Interstate*, a book-length poem about leaving my father and setting out on her own. In one of the poems, she describes settling in Portsmouth:

another place

pigeons putter by a curb
and herring gulls, starlings,
some kind of city sparrow

> just a yard full of chickens,
> mallards, white china geese

I am not rooted
but anchored, like a tug
in fog

it's not too late to begin again
this time I will make a life
solitary as a night-hunting bird
useless as an earring

Life was moving forward. At least she wasn't having to put up anymore with a defensive husband threatened by her creativity, or a boyfriend who expected her to be his housemaid.

We talked a lot on the phone during the school year. Mom would ask if we were getting to know our father better and then make us promise to visit her in the summers. I think she rationalized that Willy and I had each other and that the sibling relationship was the most important one in the long run. *Would our father give us the right attention? Were we becoming too unruly?*

We probably should have stayed in Portsmouth, for things could have unfolded nicely there. But when Mom met Arthur, she saw the promise of a life without judgment—saw a man who would never try to restrict her life in any way. The fact that Arthur wanted her to figure out how to pay for *both* their lives was what finally caused it all to unravel. She became exhausted. She had hoped that the life she'd begun to dream up in Ithaca would continue to grow in Barnstead . . . a house in the country, animals, plants, wilderness nearby.

Still, something in her life felt out of balance. Deep down she knew that this wasn't the final destination. I think she had an image in her head of where she was supposed to be, combining the ideal of a happy marriage and a kind of hippie lifestyle. Barnstead was close, Arthur was close, but they were not quite it.

SHE MUST HAVE been surprised the night she found Charter sitting at the long Press Room bar. Some inner bell must have gone off. He was long and tall, rugged, with a full beard that made him look, with his baseball cap and "Gravity Never Sleeps" T-shirt, like a cross between Abbie Hoffman and Abe Lincoln. And though he didn't look the part, he was smart like the other men, artistic. A photographer and filmmaker, he worked at an advertising firm in Exeter.

She liked him. It had something to do with his calm, a politeness bordering on chivalry. This was utterly new to her. Bill and Arthur had needed to prove themselves; like peacocks, they were always displaying their feathers. Charter was a different bird. And a few nights after that first meeting, when he picked her up and took her in his old International Harvester truck out to the woods where he lived with a community of friends and neighbors, she had the strong feeling, *This is it.*

Charter drove her down a long dirt road, passing through a forest of pine and beech that offered glimpses of a moonlit pond, into her old dream of a life. When he turned off the headlights, she stepped out into a sea of black. All she could make out were the tops of the closest pines and a sliver of moon. Charter appeared beside her, taking her arm lightly in his strong hand.

But it was his house that did it. He had built it himself, living for a year in a tree house while he put up the walls, then raised the roof with the help of carpenter friends. The place started out in the early seventies as a kind of hippie commune, friends sharing an ideology and a passion for an alternative way of life that made sense to them at the time.

The house was rustic, to say the least, with a woodstove for heat and no running water. A rough-hewn tree trunk stood in the main living area. There was a loft over the small kitchen, a discreet Buddhist altar in one corner. It was all so neat, so nicely taken care of, that my mother wanted to cry. Who was this man who lived so confidently and so lightly on this earth?

After a simple dinner of fried smelts, mashed potatoes, and garden spinach, he took her down to the Isinglass River, down a long path to a little turn in the river under a giant oak tree. He took off his shirt and stepped out of his jeans, walking into the river until he could slip under without disturbing the water. She joined him, stepping naked into the lukewarm bath. The air above the water made her shoulders and face tingle. And she knew. Knew with an inner conviction that nearly frightened her. She had finally come in off the road; she had found a home. Right away, she thought of calling up Bill and having him send the boys.

CHARTER STEPPED INTO our lives at exactly the right moment. Without him, Willy and I would have blown off course. There had been too many changes of port, too many shifts in the wind. We were just boys playing at being young men; we had no idea how to make our way in the world. Charter showed us how it was, and then he showed us what to do. *Pay attention*, he would say. *Slow down*. Neither of our parents had been good at laying down the law or sticking to a rule; Charter was the first adult in our lives with enough authority, and enough compassion, to make us listen.

When Willy and I first went to Barrington—he was thirteen, I was twelve—it took us a while to get the feel of the place. We were more than a little unhappy that first summer. Mom had moved in with this big, tall, bearded hippie and was shacking up with him in his little forest cabin. And now she wanted us to come with them?!

There wasn't enough room in Charter's house, so we slept out in a tent. There was no running water, so we either used an outhouse or pissed off the back porch. Laundry went out on the line. We showered on the front steps under a handheld watering can of warm water, and washed the dishes with hot water from the wood-stove. The rusty old pump in the back had to be primed with a cupful of water and a few quick tugs before any water came up. (When you were done, your palm would be tattooed red.)

As soon as I completed my chores, I'd grab a towel and head for the pond. After a few hours swimming and paddling the canoe around and sunbathing nude on the floating raft, I'd get restless and begin to roam the surrounding forest. My favorite path led along the southern end of Scruton Pond through a ragged wall of blueberry bushes. I kept my eyes on the dark blue water appearing and reappearing between the trees. Following the path's sharp turn, I made my way back deeper into the woods, going on until I came upon a certain granite boulder resting among the trees like an ancient asteroid. I'd scramble up onto its pockmarked face and sit atop it until my thoughts ran their course and I emptied out.

she was gone and Dad was left to oversee it. I think she had tomatoes going for a while, maybe zucchini. But no more. Since it was my dad's job to dole out the chores, invariably one of us got stuck with weeding.

I hated weeding that garden. Hated it because I hated all work that didn't feel like play, but also because I saw through it. It was a weed garden. (At least Charter's garden produced food for the table!) No matter what my father said, or how hard he emphasized the moral necessity of chores, I went to the garden reluctantly, literally dragging my heels.

I can still remember the texture of that Rocky Mountain dirt, the clumps of earth already half formed into rock. You could bust a window with a clod, no problem. (Or throw it at your brother.) It didn't so much lie on the ground as rumple it. I'd kneel down for my hour of slave labor and instantly be covered with a layer of grit, silently cursing my father for exiling me to this dried-up pigpen, this kid concentration camp with sagging wire exposed to the harsh mountain sun. But that's where I had to be, one hour minimum, weeding my father's measly garden.

Near the end of our stay at that house up in the mountains, I'd pull up clumps of weeds at random, not even bothering to get the roots. A small pile of weed tops would form outside the fence, as much dirt as plant life. I'd scratch around some more, daydreaming. Underdog nearby in the shade, waiting patiently for me to get out of prison. Now and then I'd join him. Then I'd go back to the useless task of satisfying my father. *Whatever you say, Dad.*

· · ·

When I arrived home, Mom would be in her study and Charter would be preparing dinner on the woodstove, or sitting at the table with his coffee and a newspaper. He'd sigh quietly to himself and, when he saw me standing there, look up and smile.

DURING THOSE FIRST summers in Barrington, Charter brought us along to help work on the community house, which had been constructed by the members of Scruton Pond Farm as a gathering place and all-around utility area. The idea was to expand it, opening up the space for yoga classes, dance parties, reunions. An impromptu group would meet each Saturday morning to work on putting down the new floor and erecting a new wall. Charter would set me off in a corner with a bucket of nails and show me where I needed to hammer along the wall studs.

From the start in the early seventies, the community house has always been a clear symbol of the communal principles espoused by this group of friends and neighbors. *We're in this together* was their unspoken motto. Certain jobs were shared. Together, they kept the roads cleared (or chipped in to pay for the plow guy to come and clear them), maintained the pond and dock, and helped each other when major building was needed. If anything especially important came up, the community held a meeting. Everyone voted. For instance, if someone decided to move out of the community and sell the house, the prospective buyers had to go before the community board to be approved. This was how it always had been done.

It made sense, then, that Charter would get irked when one of the original members of the group sold her house without calling a meeting and neglected to bring the buyers before the board. To him, this kind of behavior was anarchy: a flagrant and complete disregard for how things should work. As a way to protest this reckless behavior, Charter went down to the community house, measured out the area of the four walls, divided it into thirteen equal parts—one for each original membership in the community—and then painted "his" portion bright pink. If it was every man for himself, he figured, then, *Hell, I can do what I want.*

This move pissed off a lot of people. "How could you do that?" they asked. He explained his motives. No one was placated. Joyce, who lives just over the hill, and not normally a demonstrative person, went over one day and yelled at Charter for a good half hour, threatening to paint over the pink square.

The dispute died down. Months passed. A whole year. Nobody had forgotten the pink square, or its significance, but they were simply not saying anything about it publicly. However, as the date for an important community event approached and people gathered to talk about arrangements, the square became an issue again. Tempers flared. Threats to paint over the "eyesore" were renewed. Then one day Wim, the older Dutch man who lives closest to the community house with his wife Jonell, painted a two-dimensional zebra on the square. A couple of days later, he painted a goofy cow alongside the zebra. A painter and a pacifist, Wim meant to smooth things out.

You might say he was just prettifying a bold statement. But here's another way to look at it: his zebra preserved the pink flag Charter staked into the communal consciousness. Now the Dada banner had its emblem. If you walk back behind the community house today, you'll find the zebra and the cow still floating in their

field of pink. The paint has weathered a little, begun to ⌐ the heraldic animals are still staring straight ahead.

Charter laughs about it. "Water under the bridge," he s⌐ he likes to kid me about how Willy and I were scared of t⌐ and frightened at first to go swimming in the pond alone. ⌐ lived on a farm before (if Arthur and Mom's funky versi⌐ farm counted) with its array of chores. We had camped ou⌐ this was different. This was hard. Our hands and feet got ra⌐ red, our faces covered with mosquito bites, and our muscle⌐ from hauling firewood or from sanding down the addition's ⌐ floor.

When I think back on those first summers, I have to marv⌐ little. What perfect kid bliss! And kick myself for being suc⌐ wimp. But what's to do? It may have taken a while, but I ha⌐ come to appreciate the place. Over the years, I learned to apprec⌐ ate working in Charter's big vegetable garden, building a ston⌐ wall, digging an irrigation ditch. I have even come to know some⌐ thing about building a house (not much, mind you, but some⌐ thing) through helping Charter expand his abode to fit our⌐ expanding life.

⁓

I T ' S N O T E A S Y growing vegetables at seven thousand feet above sea level, especially if you don't know what you're doing. Sharon had known something. It was her idea to start the garden, but now

DAD WAS PLAYING league basketball back then, as well as competitive racquetball. He was in his mid-thirties, handsome, admired by his students. He was fast becoming what they called a "famous poet" (an oxymoron, my father once happily pointed out). With two new books of poems out, first *Rising & Falling*, then *Flood*, he was now considered at the forefront of American poetry (at least that's what it said on the book jackets). His work was included in many of the anthologies, and he got asked to read at universities across the country.

He was busy playing the academic game, too, earning more money at each position, being offered longer and longer contracts. From jobs at Wells College, Cornell, and Emerson College, to the Iowa gig and now this tenure-track position at the University of Colorado, he was making a name for himself. Within months, he'd be offered a position at the University of Washington.

He had a wide circle of friends—many of them, I later learned, well-known writers. One semester, he helped persuade his friend Richard Hugo to teach in his department at the university. They often took long car rides up into the mountains or watched weekend baseball games together. Hugo, a notorious lover of ice cream, would tease my father about his sophisticated tastes. "You probably like really good vanilla," he'd chide. "I was very consciously discriminating in those years," my father writes in the essay "Butterscotch Ripple." Hugo's teasing retort: "I like it when you take some glop and some ice cream and swirl it all together."

The next semester, the poet W. S. Merwin arrived with his knapsack on his shoulder. He came with his girlfriend, Dana, and after a brief stay in our basement, they moved even further up in the mountains. I remember visiting them up at their bungalow the following summer for a Fourth of July celebration—eating some-one's five-alarm chili and watching the fireworks explode over the jagged peaks of the Rockies.

Sharon came back that last summer in Boulder to help Dad pack for Seattle. She had been in our lives for many years now and had become more or less our stepmom. But Willy wouldn't listen to her, and I was never sure what to call her. For his part, Dad seemed jealous of my connection to Sharon and went so far as to discourage our hanging out together alone. There's a poem of Sharon's from her first book, *Salt Air*, about my father. It's called "The Same River Twice":

I am leaving, I put on my earring,
shape of a silver fish.
I am leaving, I put on my red hat
with no flower.
I put on one sock in a hurry.
I wash my face wearing my hat.
I button my blouse
over my breasts. I unbutton one button,
but you are by the window.
Half the irises are blooming.
I look in my purse and in my pocket
and in my hand. What can I do
without? My shoes are ahead of me,
pointing out the door.

When I think of Sharon I think of that poem. I think, too, of her watching us play basketball from the kitchen window, angrily washing the dishes my father ignored. The warm attention she gave to me. I think I was always a little in love with Sharon. I wanted my father to marry her and let us have a real stepmom. For them to have a kid and for me to be an older brother.

Our move to Seattle should have been exciting. We were moving to a big city, weren't we? And soon I'd be in high school with Willy, old enough to join him on his escapades. Sharon and Dad would finally figure things out, finally get married. We'd start new. Right? But it wasn't exciting. We dreaded the move. Willy resented being pulled out of his new school, I didn't want to be pulled away from yet another new best friend, and Sharon wasn't sure she wanted to go through the same old routine.

My father? I don't know what he was thinking, if he worried about the new move, or how his sons would take it. I imagine he was looking forward to the chance to step away from all the entanglements he'd created for himself. Already I had become aware of the gap between what I wanted our life to be and what it actually was. I packed my bags and hoped for the best.

Bachelor Life

> I'd hear you on the stairs,
> an avalanche of sneakers, and then the sift
> of your absence and then I'd begin to rub
> the house like a lantern until you came back
> and grew up to be me, wondering how to sleep
> in this lie of memory unless it be made clean.
>
> WILLIAM MATTHEWS, "Housework"

I'M A FRESHMAN in high school. It's our second year in Seattle. One day my brother comes home and announces that his name is "Bill." He has recently begun a disappearing act, passing over a wall I cannot scale. He's out chasing girls. Old and arthritic Underdog has just died, and Sharon has moved to a one-bedroom apartment down the hill. Our house is big and empty and, once again, underheated. More often than not, I am left to my own devices.

Here's the routine. Dad leaves a note saying he'll be home by seven. I start expecting him around six-thirty. When he's not home by seven-thirty, eight, I become stricken with a strange inertia that keeps me from doing anything useful; moving restlessly like a caged leopard, I end up in the front hall. I pass into the dining room, then drift through the hall into the living room. Then back again: hall, kitchen, dining room.

It's now eight-thirty and I am nearly wild with loneliness. My resources are exhausted. For something to do, I place an end table in the center of the hallway and arrange candles and small objects on its surface. I pick out one of Dad's ashtrays, an onyx doodad from his desk, a Bob Marley album, an empty wine bottle. When Dad finally walks in at nine-fifteen, I am waiting for him, kneeling behind the table. His arrival has been preceded by the swipe of headlights through the living room windows, the hollowed-out slam of the car door, then his hand on the doorknob, turning.

More than two hours late, he doesn't say anything. Doesn't stop to ask what I am doing in the hall, crouched behind a makeshift altar, why his stuff has been arranged on a table; doesn't even stop to look closely. He just walks upstairs—surprised, no doubt, to find the ghost of his ex-wife hiding so adeptly in the form of his younger child.

WHEN WE MOVED to Seattle, into the dilapidated three-story house on Capitol Hill, we finally settled into a space that fit our lifestyle. Empty of all but the essential furniture—a stereo on every floor, a half-stocked kitchen, and an entire third floor for Dad to use as his study—the house could have easily accommodated a family of six or more. We each had our own bedroom. There were three bathrooms and a huge dusty basement in which to hide out. Heaven. I'd come home from school to an empty house and a note to take the ten-dollar bill on the table and grab a burger and fries at Dick's Deluxe on Broadway. I was no longer a kid. In this house, I had all the room in the world. Maybe too much.

Those years in Seattle perhaps best define my relationship with my father. We had become roommates, friends, drinking buddies. Old enough to participate in more facets of his adult life, I had graduated to cocktail parties and readings. I helped him prepare for his many dinner parties, at times serving as head waiter, coat check boy, and dishwasher. Somewhere along the line, I became his very own man Friday, bringing him up fresh-brewed coffee, doing the laundry, going shopping. They were my chores, yes, but it was more than that: my father had finally found someone to do his housework. I was taking care of him while he parented me.

Soon after we arrived, Dad had workers tear off the wallpaper on the dining room walls. For some reason, they left the job half finished. Plaster and wall joists peeked through, and wires hung out of the wall where the sockets used to be. Two years later, the mess remained. My father simply pushed a long sideboard in front of the biggest holes. For dinner parties, we dimmed the lights especially low.

All through high school I slept under my father's study. Every night I'd drift off to the faint pounding of his Selectric typewriter, to the flowing bass of a jazz record. On nights when I couldn't sleep, home late and tanked on espresso, I'd make my way up the carpeted stairs and take my seat by the bookshelf in the corner. While Dad composed and revised his poems, I would listen to his records, read books off the shelf, try out my own awkward poems on his trademark yellow typing paper. We had a terrific view of downtown Seattle from our third-floor perch—of the Space Needle, of Puget Sound, the Cascades off in the distance. Below us, rows of houses gave way to the neon lights of Broadway Avenue. Dad would open a bottle of wine, turn up the heat, flip the disc, and we'd settle in.

He was listening to jazz back then, with some Marley and Dylan mixed in. Mostly late bop and cool jazz—Coltrane, Miles' *Kind of Blue*, Stan Getz's *Sweet Rain*, the Jazz Messengers, Mingus' *Ah Um*,

Monk's solo stuff, *Art Pepper Meets the Rhythm Section*. I got my ear for jazz those nights, turning over the LPs carefully at the end of each side, doing my best not to smudge the vinyl. Over time, I became familiar with the songs, began forming strong desires for specific pieces. I'd go on jags. For a while, all I wanted to hear was Monk doing "'Round Midnight," then it was Getz and Gilberto's "Girl from Ipanema." Mingus' "Better Git It in Your Soul" held me captive for nights on end, trouncing me with its incessant, swelling tsunami of a melody.

Then, when I discovered Dylan's *Blood on the Tracks*, that was all I wanted to hear—forever. Dad seemed equally possessed by the album. When "Idiot Wind" came on, he'd invariably walk over and turn the sound up, belting out along with Bob, "I can't help it if I'm lucky."

Sometimes Dad would hand me a copy of one of his poems straight out of the typewriter, and I'd sit there and ponder it a while. I even showed him my first "real" poem, which was about taking Underdog out for late night pee prowls. My father uncoiled out of his typewriter hunch, lit another Marlboro, and then read the poem, hand up at his mouth, fingers stroking his mustache. When he handed it back to me, he leaned back for his wine and said, "Keep at it."

It was the work—the romance of it—that I learned from my father. Smoke hung on the ceiling. Wine and coffee running through my veins. Jazz flowing, everywhere and nowhere at once. I soaked it up like a plant taking in sunlight.

. . .

WHEN I WAS a junior in high school, brother Bill fresh off to college, my father suggested that we move to New York City. He promised he'd get me into a private school. We'd start over in Manhattan. I begged him to let us stay in Seattle, wanting badly to get through high school with the same group of friends. I liked Seattle and the small-city-on-the-cusp-of-big-things feel it exuded. (This was the early eighties, the Boeing era, pre-grunge, years before the ascendancy of Starbucks and Microsoft.) Besides, it felt like my right. I had followed my father—and my mother, for that matter—through all the moves, all the changes of partners, the new jobs, and now I wanted a say in what we would do. Luckily for me, he respected my situation and my wishes. And, for once in my life, we stayed put.

Kind of. As he often did, my father made plans to go away for a week to teach a master class. He wanted one of his University of Washington graduate students to stay with me—not so much to baby-sit as to keep me company. Something like this had been arranged before. To me, it was always a nice change of pace, a chance to skip school.

The way it went, I came home one day to find my dad's poetry workshop in our living room. My father took me aside and told me I could choose whomever I wanted. I was not entirely sure what he meant by this. They'd all agree to stay, he was sure, so it was my choice. I caught on.

With class officially over, the group was hanging out in the living room, talking self-consciously about ideas they only half understood, beers in hand. I let my father introduce me. A pretty, dark-haired woman caught my eye. She was large-boned, soft in the shoulders. Her hair fell over her eyes, and when she shifted her head I saw that she was smiling at me warmly. I could tell she wore shirts and sweaters to hide her breasts. As I left the room, I looked at my father, nodded over to the woman, and mouthed, "Her."

A few days later, Dad heads off for his gig. An after-school note on the kitchen table tells me to meet the new "house-sitter" at her place in the University District. There's a check for a hundred dollars to cover food. The grad student is on the phone when she opens the door. She smiles and nods me in, retreating to the living room to finish the call. I look around the place, impressed by its new-wave decor. The Heckle and Jeckle salt and pepper shakers. She comes back in with a look on her face that's familiar to me as the poet's son. She's not seeing me. She's seeing a version of my father.

When we go shopping, I'm the one who puts the imported beer in the cart. She gives me a quick side glance, then returns to our list. Halfway down the aisle, she adds a couple of bottles of wine to the cart.

"Nice choice," I tell her.

That night, after dinner, we open the wine. I let her play my father's records. She lingers at the bookshelves. When I take her on a tour of the house, she wants to see my father's study. I show her the third floor, the great view down onto the city. More wine, more music. It's not long before we end up kissing on the couch. Then I take her hand and walk her downstairs to my father's room.

"This we shouldn't be doing," I say.

"Right you are," she says, her breath catching.

We stretch out on his king-size bed and stare at each other awhile.

"What am I doing?" she asks.

"I am not exactly sure," I answer.

"Touch me," she says, taking off her shirt. Who am I to argue?

Our week together goes by in a dream. I skip school two days in a row. She writes me a note for school, I forge my father's signature, and when my friends call I make excuses about relatives being in town. Free to be bad, we spend the days downtown at the museums, go to matinees on Broadway. Having returned to the store for more wine, we stay in and cook wild, unruly stir-fries in my father's wok. Most of the time, we're up on the third floor, blasting music and making out. In bed, I am too afraid, too unsure, to make love to her. I give her long massages instead, and go down on her. When she comes, her whole body shakes. When I slide back up, she holds me tight and strokes my hair.

I go back to school on Friday and when I come home she is gone. Only a note thanking me for a wonderful week. Although we've washed the sheets and all the wineglasses are free of our fingerprints, I can still smell her on my clothes. Later, we run into each other at B&O Espresso. She's with this guy, obviously a boyfriend. She gives me a hug, but I can tell she's embarrassed to introduce me. I tell the guy she tutored me in school. He gives me this funny look, but I can tell he wants to buy it. As I leave, she throws me a secret smile. I don't want to blow her cover, so I just toss them both an insouciant schoolboy wave and make for the door.

I always wanted to ask my dad if he hooked me up with the baby-sitter on purpose. If he was giving me—and her—some sort of prize. I can't believe he was fully aware of what he was doing. How could he have been? By providing me such access, he was making me complicit in a life lived on the edge of control. At least in a metaphoric sense, he was inviting me into his bed. I wanted to ask him about it, sure, but never got up the nerve.

———

AUGUST 1982. MY first summer on the mountain. I'm sixteen, up for a long weekend, visiting my father at Bread Loaf. In a few days, I'll turn seventeen and be back in Seattle for my senior year of high school.

Breakfast is out. I'm in a circle of adults clutching steaming cups of coffee. In the background, Bread Loaf Mountain (which actually does resemble a loaf of bread) sits wrapped in a morning overhang of clouds. The grass is wet with dew. It's my first morning here, my first look at the place in daylight, and I'm not sure what to make of it. It feels like I have walked into a corny movie, say *Somewhere in Time*, where the young lover wills himself back into an earlier century as a guest at a posh resort.

A bell rings in the distance and people end their conversations, putting down books and rising up out of chairs as if enacting a timed drill. My dad comes over and explains that the first workshops of the day will soon be starting. He asks me where I want to go. I have no idea. It is my father's second year on staff, so I trust his judgment.

"You could come to mine, if you'd like," he says. "Or maybe you should go to John Gardner's."

Except for my high school reading of *Grendel*, I know little of John Gardner.

"He's worth it," Dad assures me, pointing out a long, low building off in the distance. "It'll be held in there."

I make my way over to the building known to everyone as the Little Theater. It is here where all the readings are performed, where Robert Frost himself once stood to read his poems. I peer through one of the screen doors that line the building and wait for my eyes to adjust to the gloom. The lecture is beginning.

Slipping inside as inconspicuously as possible, I take a seat in the back. A man with a mane of white hair and wearing an old wool sweater leans against the stage beside a podium. He is cradling a pipe in a way that makes him look more like a fisherman than my idea of a writer or a teacher. Students are waiting in a semicircle, leaning forward expectantly. Someone has obviously asked a question, but Gardner is taking a long time to answer. He puffs on his pipe instead, appearing to mull it over. He is a short man but powerfully built. Even in repose, he is intense, seemingly capable of bursting at any moment into violent, passionate action. Then, with surprising energy, he pushes off from the stage and starts pacing in front of the startled students. Another short pause and then he answers.

I could tell right off that Gardner was a great teacher by the way the students listened so intently. The room was charged with the willed intelligence of minds trying to keep pace. I don't remember what he spoke about, but I remember being held captive by his voice, being dazzled by his presence. I remember him reciting snippets of poetry. I remember the quality of light in the room, which dropped in swaths diagonally over the rows of wooden chairs, thick with dust and pollen. I remember the circus-performance feel of the whole experience—the stage behind the podium, the ring of students, their rapt attention, the danger of something out of control about to happen. I remember how excited I felt observing the scene—and being a part of it.

Near the end of the hour, Gardner made what I thought to be a snide remark to one of his students, something about his politics. I could easily have missed the context; I only know there was a stunned silence. Maybe a student had said something closed-minded and Gardner was insisting on prying the mind back open. Maybe he was sacrificing the feelings of one student to prove a point, or maybe he had been drinking. I can remember clearly my own body shock and confusion. *What just happened?* Then the class ended, the circle broke up, and I walked transfixed out of that old theater into the misty Green Mountain air.

The next day I come down off the mountain, back into the less rarefied air of my adolescent life. Stepping onto that bus doesn't carry a triumphant sense of having stumbled into some new realm. I experience simply that old *missing out* feeling I have grown up with—missing out on my brother's escapades, on the adult world down below with its clinking glassware and laughter and rock-and-roll. Always I must go upstairs to bed. *Next summer,* I tell myself, *I'll come for the whole conference.* I will sit up in that first row, maybe even ask the great man a question.

John Gardner dies a few months later, lost in a motorcycle crash that, according to the gossip, may or may not have been an accident. I hear about it from my father upon returning home from school. He is clearly shaken, burdened by the weight of the news. There's no way it was a suicide, I tell him. That man was too alive,

I say. It's incredibly unfair. The following summer I do indeed stay the whole two weeks on the mountain and watch as the entire conference grieves Gardner's passing. At dinner, people stand up and sing "Amazing Grace" in his honor. And I remember stepping out of the inn that night, crossing over to the stone wall, and looking out over the field that runs lazily down to the Battenkill River. And I remember wanting badly to be a writer, so much so my head felt like it was about to burst.

In my sepia-tinged memory, it's my father who reads that night, though it could just as easily have been somebody else. Tim O'Brien in his trademark Red Sox cap telling us his war stories. Or John Irving holding court for two hours, reading scenes from *The Cider House Rules* that have people fainting in the aisles. Or Nancy Willard, dressed like a Blakean angel, or the poet Howard Nemerov, with his cropped white hair and his farmer's jacket looking for all the world like Frost's ghost.

But this night it's my father. I can see him clearly at the podium. He's so tall he has to lean down to the microphone. He's got his reading glasses in one hand, and he's fussing with his loose sheaf of poems. When he looks up at the audience, it's as though he is surprised to find them still sitting there. Another long silence and then he introduces the poem: each word chosen carefully and glasses put on theatrically. His is the timing of the pundit, the stand-up comic. And now he starts to read the poem, taking off the glasses, right hand dancing them in the air. The pointing finger of his left hand marking his place.

And I can see myself clearly, too. I am the tall, thin young man in the corner seat of the back row. My back is straight, my hands are on my knees in the posture of meditation. I am held fast in the magical cadence of my father's voice—by his dancing hands—by the night breeze coming in through the porous screen doors. I am taking it all in. Later, when everyone is dancing and drinking in the barn, I pass across the darkened field to the Little Theater. Taking my position behind the podium, I begin. "I am going to read three poems," I tell the phantom audience. "The first poem bears an epigraph from . . ."

$\sim$

IN HINDSIGHT, I see that my father paid dearly for agreeing to stay in Seattle. A hailstorm of grief and harm came raining down on his head. (Though, of course, he brought it on himself.) He probably saw the storm coming and tried his best to move out of its way. For my dad, moving had meant—and would always mean—opportunity, a chance to leave behind "dead ends, shames, bad times." His lifestyle both created and supported this propensity toward restlessness. As a poet-for-hire (he used to call himself "Mr. Lives on Other People's Money"), and as an itinerant master teacher of the craft, he would travel the country giving readings, lectures, workshops. There were also countless part-time gigs and readings, the summer retreats in Italy, the Bread Loaf job, the writer's residencies in Ireland, the guest visits to Israel, Budapest. Partly out of financial necessity, partly out of habit, he had spent much of his adult life on the road.

It's no accident that a good number of my father's poems were set in hotel rooms or in the single rooms of writers' conferences ("Writer-in-Residence," "The Rented House in Maine," "Toasts to the Rented House in Polgeto," "Le Quatre Saisons, Montreal, 1979.") He traveled well. He loved the simplicity of focus it took to live out of a suitcase. He appreciated the loneliness of hotel bars and airports, he enjoyed eating out and meeting friends at restaurants and jazz clubs, and he reveled in the anonymity travel afforded, those small moments of grace that befall you when you are alone in a strange city.

But he was also a homebody, someone who thought of himself as a domestic person. He writes in "Durations," one of his few truly autobiographical essays:

> I cooked for and made a home for my sons for their junior high school and high school years, in addition to the usual fatherly activities. I'm a reader, a listener to music, a man made happy by kitchen chores and pleased when there are friends at my table.

My father kept trying to make a home but never could keep from having one foot out the door.

"IN THOSE YEARS first Bill and then Sebastian left home for college, and I found myself depressed, more deeply rootless than I'd ever admitted to myself, and ricocheting around like a squash ball," my father writes in "Durations." He goes on: "I had, like many a parent, described my life as organized around and given over to my children . . . I had to begin admitting how poorly I knew me. What did I want? I had almost no idea."

What he didn't write in that essay (and never once discussed with me) was how his private and professional lives fell apart during those last few years in Seattle. How Sharon left him for good, fed up with his halfhearted commitment, his infidelities. How troubles brewing at the University of Washington finally boiled over when a female student brought charges of sexual misconduct against him.

This was happening at the start of my senior year, though at the time I was blissfully ignorant of the whole affair. I was busy chasing girls, playing on the tennis team, and coediting the high school newspaper. I had started looking into colleges—already leaning toward Pitzer College, where my brother was starting his sophomore year. I worked at a neighborhood café most nights and spent my afternoons and weekends practicing with the team or hanging out with my friends. I didn't have time to notice that my father's life was crashing down around him. And he certainly wasn't letting on.

That leaves me, years later, to piece things together on my own. I know from talking with Sharon that he was warned about sleeping with his students. I know that he couldn't stop himself. Was he a sex addict? A compulsive womanizer? I don't know. At the time of the trouble, my father held the Roethke Chair at the University of Washington, arguably one of the top poetry jobs in the country. At the relatively young age of forty, he was a senior guy there. He was set. So why did he risk ruining everything he had worked for for the sake of a few doomed affairs? Did he think he could continue sleeping with his students and not get in trouble?

It bothers me. Was his behavior toward women—at its core, obsessive-compulsive—truly an illness? Was he, as one friend described him, "a profoundly conflicted man who seemed to need to be caught"? Or was it more than just about the fucking? I approach his friends and ask them questions. One writes back in a letter: "He couldn't help making women fall in love with him." Another surmises over the phone: "If there were enough women who loved him, someone would be there to take care of him." Still another, fondly: "He was just a lonely romantic." Really, I don't know what to think.

All I know is that one day my dad showed up at Sharon's apartment, sat on the sill of one of her living room windows, and said, "We have a problem." He told her that he'd been charged with sexual harassment and might be fired. Sharon didn't understand at first. She knew about the warnings, how several students complained after he slept with them and then dropped them. This was before there was an office of sexual harassment. A friend and colleague of Dad's had worked hard to save his job, and the department simply held on to the complaints, warned Bill within an inch of his life, and kept it all quiet.

But then Dad admitted that they had a recent complaint—a student with a history of mental instability who told him she'd get even if he left her. He left her. By then the university had a ferocious sexual-complaint ombudsman. My father had resigned in an attempt to avoid having the whole thing made public. But now that the student was suing, people were coming out of the woodwork. Suddenly any student who had ever slept with my father decided to speak out against him. And there seemed to be a lot of them.

As a way to escape the strain, my father accepted an offer to be a visiting writer at the University of Houston for a semester. And though I flew down to visit him one weekend each month, I stayed in school in Seattle, and was joined by the poet Marvin Bell and his family. They moved into my house as a unit. And so for a few months I got a taste of "normal" family life—that is, breakfast on the table in the morning, packed lunches, a parent to greet me when I came home from school. Dorothy Bell became my surrogate mother. I was even an older brother, entrusted to steer Jason through the maze of my tough, inner-city high school. It was a good life but a strange one. In some dreamlike fulfillment of my childhood fantasy, I was a part of this loving, stand-in family. But where had my father gone?

When Dad came back from Houston, the student's charges had blown up into a full-fledged lawsuit. And even though his relationship with Sharon was all but officially over, he begged her to marry him. He even said he'd have a child with her. A week later he changed his mind. He began having affairs again. (I know all this because Sharon told me, years later, over cups of coffee in a Port Townsend restaurant. It had come as a shock to me, but when I told my brother about it he seemed nonplussed. "Oh yeah," he said, "I knew all about it. Didn't you?")

The trial was drawn out, longer than most murder trials, and was even briefly in the paper. Dad had moved to New York City by then, following his old friend Russell Banks to Manhattan, flying back to Seattle monthly to talk with his lawyers. The trial ended in a hung jury—nine for acquittal, three to convict. The student's lawyer wanted to pursue it, but the law firm said they would fire her if she did.

It was an ugly mess—a circus, really—shaming and hurtful to my father. His whole world collapsed on him. His reputation, already besmirched, was now tarnished seemingly beyond repair.

Who was going to hire him? I know now from talking with his friends, and by reading his essays, that it was the lowest point in his adult life. How could it not be? If I had been paying attention, or had known what to look for, I'd surely have seen the signs. The rings under his eyes. The empty wine bottles piling up in the basement. The dilapidated state of our house. Even so, I am not sure what I could have done. My father and I finished off our sad tenure in that old house, two bachelors running out a string of bittersweet days. I went off to college in Southern California, following my brother to Pitzer. Released, Dad headed for New York. Finally, he could return to the city in which he had spent so many wide-eyed nights as a young jazz fanatic—sitting at the bar of the Showplace, in the back at the Half Note.

Did my father refuse to let me in on the difficult aspects of his life out of a sense of decorum? Or was he simply unable to make the disclosure? Either way, it's a disturbing omission. To write about this now is both to add a dimension to the truth and to betray my father's careful silence.

Homecoming

Here's to the body, then, our only real estate,
our squander, our hoard. Long may it contend.

WILLIAM MATTHEWS,
"Toasts to the Rented House in Polgeto"

M Y FATHER'S FIRST apartment in New York City was this depressing little hole-in-the-wall lost in the verticality of a Stuyvesant high-rise. It was a gray, boxy thing with little or no light. "Not a fit place to wash a rat in," as Nora Joyce once said of James' flat. He stayed there a year until he got a temporary place on West 106th (also known as Duke Ellington Boulevard, he liked to point out): one of those shotgun apartments that ran back in a train of rooms. You had to walk through one to get to the next. Because the floors slanted, and because there was always something rattling in the building or somebody pounding on the walls, there were times when it felt like you were on a moving train.

My father sets a poem in that first Upper West Side apartment. It's called "Little Blue Nude." In it, the speaker (and here I picture my father raising an eyebrow, an ironic smile spreading down his face from eyes to pursed lips) has just been robbed. What makes matters worse is he knows who did it and, as the poem spills itself out in controlled confession, exactly how and why:

. . .The mere pressure of my key
in the lock, before I'd even turned it, swung my door
open and my body knew he'd come in through

the kitchen but left like a guest by the front door.
Tony, my dumpster-diving neighbor . . .

At the start of the poem, my father is sitting alone at his desk, lost in thought (in mid-ponder, perhaps, on the brutal expediencies of loss). Then, as if coming out of a fog, he fixes his scattered attention on the eponymous postcard taped to the wall—Renoir's *Little Blue Nude*. In a wishful bit of projection, he imagines her in a reverie, as if "listening to beloved music." The song he chooses for her is Ellington's 1940 recording of "Cottontail." He's choosing it for himself, of course, as a kind of twice-removed sound track "you could turn to . . . not as a mood- / altering drug nor as a consolation, but because / your emotions had overwhelmed and tired you." By doing so, of course, he's already begun reclaiming what Tony has taken from him.

A little farther along, the speaker returns to the song:

. . . when Ben Webster kicks into
his first chorus, they're back, all your emotions,
every one, and in another language, perhaps
closer to their own.

He's pulling himself out of an emotional black hole. And he's doing it with music, with the spark of an image on a postcard (sent by a friend? a lover? a son?). By stringing together this utterance, word by word, he's begun reweaving a tapestry. He's using Webster's great torrent of musical decisions to bring him back to the land of the living.

In one of his essays on literature in *Burning Down the House*, Charles Baxter states that "traumatized people tend to love their furniture." By this he means, I think, that we turn in times of soul crisis to the very things we've invested ourselves in. For my father, his books and his music collection were his figurative La-Z-Boy. They were the sanctuary for his inner life. My father surrounded himself with the things he loved—books, music, wine, art. They were the totems of his habits, which, in turn, were the ritual tools of his art making. They made him up. They were extensions of his family, his past, his body, his inescapable foibles. His emotional life contained in static animation.

Before the robbery, Tony asked him why he was listening to jazz:

"Are you writing a book on jazz or what?"

Matthews looks over at his cassette collection:

"No, I said, I just love these."

. . .

But that conversation explains why
he took the tapes and left the typewriter.
Writing is my scam, he thought, and music my love. . . .

Other neighbors ask what he's working on all those late nights of typewriter clatter. His belated answer:

It's a reverie on what I know, and whom,
and how I manage to hold on to them.

Of course, it's also his reverie on trying to find, and hold on to, a new home.

THOSE FIRST YEARS in Manhattan must have been hard for my father. He was broke, busted by the lawsuit, without steady work. Physically, he was a wreck. He was smoking too much, drinking too much, staying up late at night, and burning himself out on the road, giving readings to make extra money. He was depressed, exhausted, guilty. (Did he feel that he had gotten what he deserved in Seattle?) His friends worried about him and did their best to help him out, but most university hiring committees at the time wouldn't even consider him. In a sense, he'd been blacklisted from the academic world he had grown up in.

To his credit, my father refused to give up. Instead, he gathered himself together and moved on, picking up work when and where he could. He taught John Ashbery's class at Brooklyn College when Ashbery was on sick leave and accepted Columbia University's offer to cover spare classes here and there. He took on a variety of visiting writer stints, read anywhere that would have him. When Mark Mirsky gave him part-time work at the City College of New York, whether he knew it or not, William Matthews started back on the path to respectability. *Nice work if you can get it.*

My father went to New York to get down to the essential work of living his adult life. He came to get his creative work done. And he came to be reborn. But he also came for the culture. Here he is again in "Durations":

All those languages overheard on the streets, and all the dialects of English! The restaurants seemed to include every possible cuisine, and though I couldn't afford most of them, it pleased me to think they were there, the way I had been excited on my first visits to the public library in Troy. All those books, and I might read any of them.

Like countless artists before him, my father had both left home forever and come home. He didn't state this directly. He was being cautious. For he knew that the only thing certain in the life of the poet-for-hire is migration. But those last years were a different story. My father once said of his old friend Richard Hugo, "He was always homing." The same could be said of him. New York City became my father's true home, his center, the hub from which he began a new phase of travel. "To travel is to engage the fantasy that one can be at home anywhere," he writes in the essay "Travel." But now when he went out on the road—to give readings, to visit friends, to vacation—he also knew he had a place to return to.

It helped that my dad's sister, Susan, lived in Manhattan—a long subway ride downtown to the West Village. After years of living across the country from each other, they were finally together in the same city. If nothing else, it made it easier for their mother to fly over from England; they could take turns putting her up in their guest rooms. But it was more than that. Artists and teachers both, they were refugees from a shared childhood and exiles from the tame Midwest of their birth. It was one of the pleasant surprises of my father's adult life to have escaped to New York only to rediscover his family there.

He had friends living nearby, too, and a parade of old students stopping by on their visits to the city. Once a year, he'd meet with his three best buddies for an epic night of fine food, wine, and the raucous, roundtable discussion among friends and writers. There's a photo of my father with these three—the poet Stanley Plumly, the novelist Russell Banks, and the poet and editor Daniel Halpern. They are all sitting on a couch, arms wrapped around each other's shoulders. Everyone in the shot is laughing, their heads thrown back and mouths open. And though there's a slight awkwardness, a stiffness that comes with a group portrait of self-conscious writers, there's also something free and alive in their expressions—a kind of wild excitement you see on the faces of kids on amusement park rides. These men are thrilled: to be in each other's company, to be friends, to be photographed together. They were indeed a boys' club, a charmed circle of friends.

My guess is that my father's friends didn't judge him harshly for his troubles in Seattle, or for his womanizing in general, but that he felt they would. I think at different times and in different ways they tried to get through to him. They were certainly encouraged when he started going to therapy. But my father was a private, secretive man. And the fierce loyalty he carried for his male friends—and that they held for him in return—must have complicated matters. In moments of crisis, you do whatever it takes to defend your loved ones. My father leaned on his friends.

Now teaching full-time at City College, he enjoyed the walks uptown into Harlem and appreciated the returning adult students he taught there—students who seemed to draw from deeper wells for their poetry than the young hotshots straight out of college. Every year or so, he'd also guest-teach for Columbia's writing pro-

hotel, with the John Bunch Trio providing the jazz, and an open bar. The photographs show a beaming couple holding up flutes of champagne. My father towers over his bride, but he's looking down at her playfully. And she's beaming back up at him. There is also a picture of the Matthews men together for the first time in years—my brother, my dad, and me. Drinks in our free hands and arms draped over each other's shoulders, we're smiling in a confident, easy manner. "Hope" is the unwritten caption under the snapshot. It could be crossed out, replaced by "Wait and See."

—◆—

A COUPLE OF YEARS go by. It's after my sophomore year in college, and I'm back up at Bread Loaf for the first time as a real contributor. Though my father is still on the faculty, he has been steering clear, allowing me room to be more than just Bill Matthews' son. I appreciate this. With a handful of inspiring college English classes under my belt, I want to see if I can make it along this path on my own.

I've just had my first story workshopped. The class hates the piece. I've been reading too much Borges, they tell me. The story is a badly plotted rip-off of García Márquez. If not for a lone affirmative response—I see promise, is the generous way one of the workshop leaders put it—I would have been trampled in an elephant herd of derision. I spend the afternoon licking my wounds

gram, teaching classes on Freud, Nabokov, Dante, and Martial's epigrams. He was translating again—mostly Martial but also some contemporary Hungarian poets. And, after three years, his seventh book of poems, *Foreseeable Futures*, was published by Houghton Mifflin.

When he finally settled into what would be his last residency— a co-op apartment on 121st between Broadway and Amsterdam— my father stowed his scuffed suitcases and sagging, triple-taped boxes down in the musty storage room. ("I have had thirteen domiciles," he writes. "Thirteen sets of change of address notices mailed, thirteen massive packings and unpackings of books, thirteen new phone numbers, etc.") After years of hard travel— gradually, the way an adult learns an instrument later in life by clearing away the clutter of habit—my father started to trim back his possessions. Once a year, in a form of emotional spring cleaning, he'd purge himself of the random stuff he had accumulated. He threw out correspondence, gave clothes to Goodwill, sent books to libraries or passed them on to his students. (I remember packages arriving unannounced on my doorstep in recycled mailers out of which invariably spilled reader's copies, journals, and jazz cassettes recently replaced by CDs.)

Always a composite of his habits—reader, smoker, drinker, listener of good music—my father was now also a Metropolitan Opera season ticket holder, a Knicks fan. Almost by accident, in ways he could never have expected, he was happy in his life. He'd become a New Yorker.

·   ·   ·

ARLENE WAS IN my father's life at this point, *was* his life—his first serious partner since Sharon. She was great for him, everyone agreed. She relaxed him. They connected through humor and a mutual love of cooking. A book editor at Villard, Arlene soon began studying to become a psychoanalyst. Tiny in build, with wild curly hair. Almost manic in energy. She wasn't an intellectual, but she was smart and street-savvy and tough. Not needy in the least. And she adored him.

I remember one dinner at the apartment. I was visiting over winter break, and the whole day had been spent preparing a holiday meal. There were plans to go see the latest Woody Allen flick, *Hannah and Her Sisters*, or to stay home and turn on the Knicks game. Dad was busy in the kitchen with some elaborate dessert; Arlene and I were in the dining room setting the table.

This was our first real time alone together. And though I felt comfortable in Arlene's presence, I didn't know what to say to her. She spoke first.

"Your old man loves you, you know that?"

"I guess," I said.

"He talks about you all the time."

I continued to lay out the forks.

"You and your brother are the best thing in his life. He says that. Just don't forget that, okay?"

I wasn't sure why she was saying this to me, but I wanted to give something back of equal significance, something that told her I saw what she had done for my father.

"You might have knocked us out of the top spot."

She laughed, acknowledging the exaggeration but not taking offense.

"Well, we'll have to see about that."

There are no out-and-out love poems in *Foreseeable Futures*, the 1987 book that my father dedicated to Arlene. I am not sure there needs to be. The whole book is a love poem of sorts—a toast raised to a life, if not always well lived, then at least survived with grace. Throughout its pages, I see my father breathing a sigh of relief, as if looking around and appreciating the small ironies. He's just come through the most difficult passage of his adult life, and he's still standing. Not only that, but he's found a new partner, a great apartment in his beloved city; he's got work, a new book out, friends around him. His sons have grown up, gone off not to prison but college. Things are truly looking up.

Friend and fellow poet C. K. Williams says of *Foreseeable Futures*, "These are dark poems and wise poems, poems that speak with a maturity rare in our needful time." He's right. Listen as the speaker of "The Accompanist," a jazz pianist, instructs on how to provide expert accompaniment for the great singer:

Don't play too much, don't play
too loud, don't play the melody.

I can't help picturing Tommy Flanagan here, talking about years with Ella Fitzgerald. Or Mal Waldron in an interview al backing Billie. Or maybe it's the poet himself, hiding behind a sona, who is speaking so wisely about the exact difficulties rewards) of writing—and living—well.

That their wedding was so openhearted and festive was a mony to Arlene's character, and to my father's happiness company. There was an elegant ceremony in a small m

down by the river. Though I skip dinner, I finally screw up the courage to go to the night's big dance in the barn.

A handful of beers later and I have come to rest on this hill. After a night of dancing seduction, I am sprawled in one of Bread Loaf's forest-green Adirondack chairs, come to clear my head, to drink beer, to witness the night sky's fireworks of stars. I am not alone. Before me stands the Hill Roller. Behind: her father, tied into a circle of conversation on the front lawn of a large white house. The talk is of experience. Of this trip, that catastrophe. Of children going off to school and of ideals lost somewhere in among the boxes of the last move. But I am only half listening, my heart already lost to the Hill Roller.

Unafraid, she rolls down into the landscape of faded color and deepening shadow, emerging from the dark at the lip of the hill like some pagan goddess, illuminated by the moon's widening swath of silver-tinged, reflected light. How old is she? Nine? Ten? It doesn't matter. She rolls a lithe, loose, spiraling string of lop-sided circles down the hill. When she reaches the bottom, her arms and legs sprawling out slowly in a sigh, she starts back up again. She does this over and over—flop on the ground, roll, come to rest, then up for more. After each roll, her smile grows larger, her eyes more gleeful.

Me? I am lonely in that melodramatic way eighteen-year-olds often are, burned a little from standing too close to the fire, uncomfortable in a skin made maddeningly alive by the incessant licks of the wind. What am I doing on this hill? I *was* waiting for something to happen, placing myself in the most likely spot lightning might strike. I *was* hoping to get laid. Now I don't know. Still sweaty from the dancing, I am body drunk from the keg beer and heart drunk from the memory of the beauty I was dancing with. How she mouthed "Let's Get It On" in my ear before suddenly slipping off to the bathroom and, rumor had it, disappearing with the famous novelist notorious for snaring young things in the net of his passionate intelligence.

On my way out to this lonely outpost, I passed the infamous Tequila Taxi, an old Mercedes perpetually crammed with wild, drunken young men and women piled on top of each other like those plastic monkeys in a barrel. Cigarette smoke slipped out of the cracked open windows. They had been singing loudly and were in the middle of a stagy, inane argument over what tune to mangle next. The cheery voice of my friend Woody called out to me to join the fun. He had thrown on a British accent for a lark.

"We're partaking in tequila shots, old chum, and might you know the lyrics of any of the lesser-known songs off of *Zenyatta Mondatta?*"

Another time I'd have taken him up on his offer. I'd have jumped into the passenger seat and ridden shotgun with some pretty poet in my lap who would play geisha and drip tequila shots onto my tongue. Would have sung new-wave pop tunes until I went hoarse while Woody drove us all through the bumpy back fields in his archaic chariot, unhinged headlights illuminating the tall grass that dropped before the grille like ocean seaweed.

But not tonight. Tonight I was on a mission. I was in search of an outcropping worthy of Heathcliff, for great open spaces upon which to let free my tormented soul. And so kept walking, painfully self-aware, out into the night, taking off my shoes and passing barefoot into the dewy grass, only to be disappointed by the crowd of adults huddled at the top of the hill. I wanted epic solitude. I wanted the stars to realign themselves into a constellation that only I could read.

AFTER A FEW minutes of listening in on the adults' hilltop conversation, I am ready to split, my thoughts already turning back to the hunt. Maybe the beauty will have spurned the great man's advances by now, will be waiting for me to join her on the dance floor. There is always hope. But when I look up from my beer, the Hill Roller is standing before me. Upright, at attention, arms straight to her sides, she is giddy, effervescent, all crooked smile and bangs. She wants me to watch her roll.

There is no choice in the matter, I can see, and so I allow her to take my hand and draw me off my seat. Propping my beer against the chair, I lie down next to her on the grass. From this vantage, my gaze comes to be directed out at the field beyond and at the mountains looming askew in the background. It feels appropriate to be lying in the cold grass, with the sky hanging over my head. Atop the closest ridge, the tops of the darkened trees are banded by a thin strip of blue-black; the furthest-off mountain wading like a gigantic cloud in an ocean of still blue sky. I want to be able to paint such intensity. To write down the precise words.

Then it hits me: the Hill Roller is the *spirit* of the raven-haired beauty. She is the literal embodiment of her sexy soul. And while the middle-aged writer is off fucking the red-blooded colt in some moldy, top-floor room, bed squeaking away and floor buckling, I am out here in the great cosmos of night, lying head to head with pure soul, a full-fledged goddess of nature, dancing a dance of grace and communion. I can almost convince myself I am getting the better end of the bargain.

The Hill Roller is off—and I with her, pushing off into the dark. I roll awkwardly, veering off to the side like a broken-down cart while the Hill Roller spirals into the dark, small grunts of pleasure drifting back to me. The adults on the hill—their circle opening out to view the spectacle—applaud as we scramble back up the slick grass. The Hill Roller and I laugh and brush each other off and, in that moment, I feel as if I know what it's like to be old, to have your body go against its best intentions. When I make it back to my chair, I am told I look like sticks being blown in the wind.

Later, the Hill Roller's father comes to claim his exhausted daughter, proud to have produced such exuberance. It is late. The circle begins to disperse. The Hill Roller comes over to give me a kiss on the hand—one last blessing—before she lets herself be picked up. Father and daughter wander off, stacked like a totem. A young couple is next to leave, arm in arm, hips knocking lightly together. Then a lone woman, beautiful to break your heart, trailing a sweater through the grass, looking back once, I swear, to see if I was coming. Then it is only me and two drunk men arguing happily. But they are heading back, too.

And then I am alone. Happy, though. I come to this understanding slowly, almost without thinking. *I'm me*, I say, or something agonizingly earnest like that, and stand up, leaving the bottle propped against the chair base. I don't need any more beer: I am young and not afraid to roll. And though the moon has slipped behind a bank of clouds, the white house is lit with assurances. My body wants to rattle like sticks in the wind. I am in love with the Hill Roller, with life, and with the night. When she is older, I will ask her to marry me.

———

DURING THE YEARS I was in college, and the two I lived in Los Angeles, I'd make it a point to visit my father in the city. I loved coming into Manhattan. When I stepped into Grand Central Station's cavernous main hall, I would imagine myself back to an earlier time, a young writer in the city to meet his editor over martinis at the Algonquin. I'd make my way through the crowd, taking as much of the scene in as I could without looking like a tourist. The doors to the shuttle would hiss open and the crowd of people around me surge through the opening: *Welcome to New York and get out of my way.*

I loved the feeling of coming up out of the subway and emerging onto the corner of Broadway and 110th; loved how, in the transitional space of a few steps, I'd cast off everything I had been up to that point and walk forward with a glowing sense of possibility only great cities can make you feel. I'd walk up Broadway in a daze, cresting at 116th and starting down into Harlem, buffeted by the wind off the river. First I'd pass the grand gates of Barnard and Columbia, then walk under the looming steeple of Riverside Church. When I made it to 121st, my father's block, I'd turn up his quiet side street and haul my bags into the lobby of his building. There'd be the brief ride with one of the doormen—weird Peck or talkative John—to the fifth floor. The knock on the door and Dad padding barefoot down the hall. That intimate moment as he undid the lock, hearing his breath, his voice saying my name. Him letting me in and us dancing an awkward two-step hug in the doorway.

The first few hours back in each other's company were always the best. Excited to be with my father again, I'd throw my bags on the single bed in the tiny guest room. (I could unpack later.) Dad would pull out the wine or brew some coffee while I played music and went through his books. We'd make plans for my stay, then I'd make calls to friends while he started dinner. We wouldn't say much, just some casual banter about what we'd been doing. I'd be between jobs, seeing someone new, trying to finish a short story.

During one such visit, my father spent the weekend making me a dozen tapes that covered the major movements and players of jazz. A birthday present, he dubbed it "The Core of Jazz." It started with Louis Armstrong and Duke Ellington but rather quickly focused in on the major saxophonists—Coleman Hawkins, Ben Webster, Lester Young, Sonny Rollins, John Coltrane. My father loved Lester so much, he made two entire tapes of his work, early and late. And there was one tape devoted to the "players," jazzmen integral to the evolution of the art but not seminal. Earl Hines, Dexter Gordon, Art Pepper, J. J. Johnson, Bud Powell.

In the middle of the marathon taping session, we went out to hear Dad's favorite pianist, Tommy Flanagan, at the Blue Note. We drank wine the first set and then ordered whiskies, sipping them down slowly through a second mesmerizing set. Flanagan capped the night off with a gorgeous version of "Some Other Spring" that magically morphed halfway through into "Easy Living." My dad heard the shift early and sat back in his chair happily, refraining from clapping. But before Flanagan had fully switched over into the new song, when it was a hybrid species, my father was already tapping out its new melody.

Sad to say, my father's marriage to Arlene came to an end during this period. I'm not at all sure what happened. My father didn't (couldn't?) tell me why things fell apart, he just said that the marriage was over. I didn't press the issue—and I wasn't around much then—and I felt reluctant to later. (I wasn't very close to Arlene, and to write about her—and her marriage to my father—seems like an invasion of privacy. Besides, as a way to protect myself, I learned to block out aspects of my father's personal life: I didn't want to know his later partners well for fear of being burned when they left.)

When my father was between marriages, we'd quickly revert to our bachelor days in Seattle. Our times together in New York were always pretty much the same. The same apartment, the same Dad. If I woke up in the middle of the night, he'd surely be typing in his study. If the fridge was empty, we'd go out for Ethiopian down the block. Dad would ask about my latest girlfriend or—for I brought my life with me like dirty laundry—I'd bore him with the melodrama of some new developmental stage I'd been stuck in.

We had the routine down. Through three official marriages and two unofficial ones, my father somehow always remained a bachelor.

Ruining the New Road

You will need pain
heaving under you
like frost ruining a new road.

WILLIAM MATTHEWS, "What You Need"

I T'S 1989. I have been on the road for four months, doing my best Kerouac imitation, most recently catching a train out of Vancouver, taking a bus down through North Dakota, and hitch-hiking into Vermont from upstate New York. I am twenty-four years old and have yet to hold down a steady job for longer than a year. The writer Charles Gaines' eerily detached description of himself in his essay "Cooking the Rat" fits me perfectly:

> . . . he will float over the country as if it were a bazaar, picking through a booth here, a booth there, for experiences. He is vain, feckless, and light, with a grandiose sense of himself that buoys and floats him over his own life. It will be years before he knows anything worth knowing.

The whole time on the road I've only called my dad once, and then to borrow money, so I am more than a little surprised when he invites me to Bennington, a summer writers' conference where he's on faculty. I am excited at the prospect of seeing him again.

He is a cool father, as fathers go, especially now that I've grown up and can hang out with him for longer periods of time. There is a lot we can talk about without having to go too deep. And he is at his best at these conferences—the beloved poet, the warmhearted, generous teacher. Who was it that said father and son did best as host and guest?

There isn't anybody around when I arrive, so I am free to take a relaxed, solitary walk around the Bennington campus, which feels more like a nineteenth-century New England farm than a college. I eventually stumble upon the main office, where a nice lady gives me a room key and a map to my "quarters." My father has been expecting me.

The afternoon swelter of a Vermont summer is bearing down, and the heavy weight of the pack gets me sweating. But I don't mind, I'm already dreaming of a long shower and a change of clothes. A snaking footpath walks me through high-grass fields (virtually dancing with grasshoppers) and then shadows the ragged edge of a pine forest, gradually upgrading to a road. After passing a row of two-story houses, one with a mysterious walled garden, I come to the last house on the edge of a freshly mown pasture. The generous branches of a huge oak tree blanket the old home's roof. I go upstairs, drop my stuff on the monk's bed, and immediately take a long, cool shower.

A half hour later, I head back out into the late afternoon, dressed in my one decent outfit and feeling as lucky, as content, as I have in weeks. After a few minutes of wandering around the barns that pass as classrooms in this place, I hear my father's melodious voice drifting down from a cracked-open window over my head. Hoping to eavesdrop, I quietly climb up the steep, switch-backing stairs.

The class is silent, busy listening and taking notes while the great poet discourses on poetry. I decide to surprise him on his way out and settle on the windowsill above the staircase, basking in the light breeze coming in the open window. A student asks about Whitman. My father clears his throat.

"Remember the children's book *Ferdinand the Bull*? Ferdinand the flower gazer is a cartoonist's poet. Whitman's a little like that: self and nature were his fascination. And in those cloverly mirrors, society gets blurred. But Whitman was more complex than a cartoon. There were many sides to his character."

Another asks, "Isn't he a bit *too* much, though? All that grandiose listing of America's charms?"

" 'I resist anything better than my own diversity,' Whitman wrote in 'Song of Myself.' His plan for it was like Oscar Wilde's for temptation: give in."

The student continues. "Yeah, but he throws it *all* in, the kitchen sink and everything. I get overwhelmed."

"That might be the point. The jazz saxophonist Zoot Sims once said of Stan Getz, 'He's a great bunch of guys,' and not altogether fondly. Like Dickinson, Whitman is a mirror. A terrifying one, perhaps. He knew us before we knew ourselves. Looking into 'Song of Myself' provides exactly the same uneasy tingle as noting in the mirror how much more we resemble our parents as we age."

After about twenty minutes, the class ends and the students start filing out. They stream down the steep steps below me, chatting to each other, exuding the familiar energy that comes from a dynamic, energizing class. Since everyone is still occupied with the lecture, along with the not-so-easy task of managing the switch-backing barn steps, no one notices me. All except, that is, a stunning young woman with green eyes who, when looking up and seeing me there, recognizes in an instant the "son."

Our gazes meet and hold briefly before she is forced to continue passing down the stairs. But before disappearing from view, she throws me a last bold look and smile. The world is in that glance. I feel attraction and the upward surge of lust and deep friendship, a little fear, and the wild excitement of recognition.

I spend that first night in my father's company. We attend a reading, then a cocktail party. Everywhere we go, admirers surround my father; he presides over each new conversation with a slightly stiff but affable grace as if he were a guide taking his listeners to the local bar. He is pleased to have me see him in his element, I can tell. And I am happy for him. Happy, in fact, with just about everything. It doesn't hurt that I keep getting *Is that the son of the famous poet?* looks from all the ladies and that the beer tap is flowing.

My father has recently remarried again. Her name is Pat. I've not yet met her. He mentioned Pat once to me in a phone call and then, a few months later, I received a postcard from the Bahamian hotel where they were honeymooning. I ask what she's like. Dad tells me that they met soon after things ended with Arlene. That she is smart, soft-spoken, giving. A divorcée, the mother of three children, a published fiction writer.

Listening to my dad describe Pat, I know that she fits perfectly the mold of my father's new women. After Sharon, my father seems to have made a conscious decision to be with women who move outside the world of poetry and academia; who, in build and temperament, resemble my mother less and less. Though a writer, and obviously bright, Pat will not in any way compete with my father professionally. She is clearly devoted to him, willing to put her own literary aspirations on the back burner.

When the conversation turns away from Pat, we slip free of the group with our beers and catch up on the *important* news: who the Knicks are going to pick up in the off-season, the best cuts off the new Dylan boxed set. Dad is back to smoking heavily, which worries me, but otherwise he looks pretty good. He seems content in his life. What can I say? When he asks about my future plans, I am embarrassed by my restless inactivity and change the subject quickly.

At some point a group of us heads out for a ramble on one of the winding back roads. Everyone talks at once, forming and re-forming into smaller groups. I have moved on ahead, away from the giddy talk. I am tired of the showing off, of the slyly competitive efforts of the students to endear themselves to their teachers. I have come to hate—and also hate in myself—the top-of-the-class wit that flies out of our mouths.

When we pass beyond streetlamps, I am joined by a woman who, slipping her arm in mine, tells me her name is Jo. She likes the way I hold myself, she tells me in a voice so hushed I must lean in to catch her words. She is in her mid-thirties, a dancer, lives in Manhattan. I like that she seems genuinely interested, and not just that I am my father's son. She asks about my travels, about what I am reading. I barrage her with questions about dance to get her to talk about her body. She's attractive in that physical, unconscious way of dancers—confident, graceful, her skimpy T-shirt hanging alluringly off her shoulders. At pauses in our talk, during a shared laugh, she lets her hand light on my hip. When the road makes a slow turn right, we meander left.

As soon as we step inside her room, I take her into my arms and kiss her. She pushes me against the wall and kisses me back. I pull off her shirt and bend down to kiss her small dancer's breasts. She pulls off my shirt and we shuffle over to the bed. I start going down on her, pulling off her skirt, but she wants me up with her. We pull the rest of each other's clothes off and start wrestling for the top position. I win, holding her arms over her head and kissing her throat. Then I push my knee between her legs and open them up slowly. Jo reaches down and guides me into her. Both of us holding our breath in anticipation. But I wilt as I go in. Then I fall out.

Jo tries to rub me back into an erection, but I roll off. She climbs onto me and sits up in a straddle. I am embarrassed and so push her away. She gives me a look of surprise and starts to move toward me seductively. All of a sudden, I'm angry. I want to shout or punch the wall, so I get out of bed and start dressing. Jo gives up, lying back down and lighting a cigarette. She tells me I'm overreacting, but I'm already heading for the door. I try to apologize, can't find the words. She tells me not to sweat it, to come back another night. I leave, walking back to my room in the dark, watching the nearly full moon plane across the tree line.

I AWAKE TO a loud knocking on my door. Before I have time to get out of bed, the beauty with the green eyes from the stairwell barges in, a cup of coffee in her hand. She introduces herself and throws my pants at my head. "We're going for a walk," she tells me. "Before your father's afternoon workshop," she adds with a laugh.

"Do I know you?"

"I already told you. I'm Elsa, the Mysterious Lady of the Stairwell. Now get dressed. We're going outside."

She scoffs at my suggestion that she wait outside while I get dressed. She doesn't even allow me to take a piss or wash my face. When I look out the window, I see that it is late morning, maybe past noon. Where is this crazy-lovely girl taking me?

As soon as we are outside, Elsa makes for a footpath that winds down in a ragged zigzag through the uncut fields. She runs with her arms held out from her sides, as if attempting to fly. My head feels only marginally attached to my body—I didn't sleep very well after the fiasco with Jo—and at every step it shatters into tiny shards of pinprick light. I have to hurry to catch her, almost losing her at the forest's edge as she ducks into the trees. Eventually I find Elsa hunched over a downed red pine, pulling off her shoes and humming to herself. I follow her lead, shivering in the forest chill and happy to be on an adventure. She hides our shoes under a bush and motions me forward through the branches.

We have said no more than a dozen words to each other and here we are holding hands and passing through a magical forest. She talks excitedly about her friends and about the light in trees, about wood elves and Yeats' trance poetry. I tell her about my days on the road, about the allure of traveling. I tell her all the stuff you say when you've become intoxicated, when you are trying hard as you can to impress the kindred spirit that has appeared at your side. She listens intently and, when I'm talked out, recites tree names and points out the wild trillium beginning to unfurl.

It is simple. Elsa is beautiful and I am in love with her ("a fool for beauty," as the old song goes). She is my grown-up Hill Roller. Her long, black hair and pale skin, her green eyes, her sharp mind, and the lithe beautiful body she stands in—they capture my romantic spirit. I lean in close to her whenever we stop walking, drink in her smell. I reach into her hair and lose myself in its softness. I kiss her as we straddle a mending wall at the edge of the forest. She doesn't resist but she doesn't kiss back either. She loves a guy back home, she tells me, and mustn't be unfaithful.

For the next few days Elsa and I are inseparable. We roam the woods like young lovers in the movies: we roll in the haystacks lining the fields, chase after the crows congregating on the main lawn, break into the walled garden. But no matter how hard I try to persuade her, she will not go to bed with me. In fact, she stops kissing me, deciding after a late night phone call back home that this, too, is inappropriate.

"No more kisses for the boy," she tells me, fingers to my kissing mouth.

And if I spend the days avoiding Jo, at night I am busy searching her out. She keeps inviting me to her room, and I keep going in. We smoke cigarettes and try another round in bed. Again the same result, but now the anger has burned off. We lie on the floor, wrapped in sheets, and I tell her all about my thing for Elsa. She laughs at me, not the least threatened.

"When are you going to tell her about your lover, Mr. Man?"

I don't want to talk about it. I want to get back to making love. Jo is more than happy to oblige.

"You're trying too hard," she tells me, sitting back with a cigarette and a kind smile. "You're all tensed up. Feel these calves, they're like rock."

She's right, of course. I *am* trying too hard. I never thought of it that way. It seemed natural to keep trying. As if by trying harder, I'll get harder.

"I think we should just let it be awhile. Take a break. We could do something else. Play cards or something. Or maybe you should try sticking it to your dream girl."

I tell her to "fuck off" and throw a pillow at her. But she's right. About it all.

THE NEXT MORNING, on one of our off-the-trail wanderings, Elsa and I come upon a flume. Half stream, half waterfall, it rises up out of the ground like an escalator of rock, moss, and spring-water. This is my first direct experience with a flume, so I stop for a moment to stare. It's as though the gods have conjured up the perfect playground for lovers—part jungle gym, part outdoor Turkish bath. Elsa is already halfway up, climbing her way through the boulder-sized rocks. I hurry to catch her and we make our haphazard way over the slick stones. At the top of the flume we come upon a small cave with a slender waterfall dropping across its mouth; we slip into the damp crawl space and sit down cross-legged on the slick ledge. The spray from the falling water glazes our faces, and the echoes of our laughter bounce around us. At Elsa's urging, I stick my head into the freezing cold current. Shout out from the sheer joy-pain of it.

On the last night of the conference, Elsa and I end up treading the lines of the basketball court in the moonlight. I am doing my best to convince her to give up her boyfriend and join me on the road, but she keeps shaking her head and pouting. Sometime after midnight, we break into the theater. We try on old costumes, moving like ghosts between the musty ropes and pulleys. Dressed as a cross between Ophelia and one of the Musketeers, she talks about being honest and faithful and open. Looking for all the world like a gay pirate, I counter her with words like "electricity," "fate," and "whim." Finally, I relent. In accordance with the maiden's wishes, I will stay her trusted friend.

When we step outside into the warm morning light, people are already getting up for the last day's activities. A few of the older women shoot me looks that tell me my poet's-son VIP pass has long since expired. (One of them, I notice with dismay, is Jo's dancer friend.) Elsa and I part ways outside her dormitory. She hesitates at the bottom step. Taking one last shot, I tell her I need some sleep before heading back out and that what I want more than anything is to go upstairs, sleep with her through the day, and wake up in her arms. She kisses me on the cheek mournfully and goes inside, turning back for one last soulful glance. Feeling like a bad dog, I slink back to my room.

After a fitful nap, I join my father for lunch. He's willing to give me a ride to his rented summer house in the Adirondacks. I can even stay there for a few days before I get back on the road. I accept his offer thankfully, in need of some quiet time away from all this distraction. But my father seems distant. He's fussing with his coffee and shooting me small looks.

"What's up, Dad?"

"It's really not my business . . ."

"I am asking your opinion, so I guess it is."

"Well, I admire your energy."

I keep my mouth shut, curious where this will go.

"But this may not be what you need in your life right now," he tells me. "This splitting of your, ah, attention."

He says "attention" with a wink in his voice, like he's being democratic.

I have half a dozen smart-ass rejoinders, but I am so shocked to hear my father giving me romantic advice that I don't know what to say.

"Maybe you should go at it one at a time."

"Okay, Dad. You're right. Is that how it works for you?"

I stand up from the table and grab my tray. Dad is glaring at me. What was I thinking? Of course he knew about Jo and Elsa. The place has been buzzing with gossip. Only Elsa seemed oblivious to the talk. And he's right, of course, but it's hard to take coming from him.

"Listen, I've got about an hour before we head off, right? Let's meet back at the car in an hour? Cool?"

Dad nods his head thoughtfully.

"Okay?"

He doesn't answer. I'm not sure what I want him to say, anyway.

"I'm outta here."

And with that, I head for the woods. When I get to the flume, I take off my clothes and climb into the pool of freezing water. I know it doesn't work this way, but I want the water to purify me. And in a way it does, for as I walk back down the path, an understanding knocks into me, chest-level: I have been following in my father's footsteps. I've tried to look like him, dress like him. He listened to Dylan and jazz, so I listened to Dylan and jazz. He stayed up late and wrote poems; I did too. And I've looked away from his transgressions. In fact, I've transferred his bad-boy behavior into my own life. Drinking, womanizing, leaving without saying good-bye. I'm sharing the world he invited me into when he helped me select that baby-sitter. But now, instead of Dad introducing me to women, I am searching them out myself.

When I get back to the car with my bags, Dad is sitting in the front seat, ready to go. We don't speak on the car ride north. I stay with him for three days and the subject never once comes up.

———◞

THE BUS PULLED into San Francisco as it started to get dark. Out on the slick streets, I looked at the smudged and crumpled map a friend had given me with directions to one of his favorite crash pads. I had to stop a few times and ask directions but after a while stumbled onto the Haight, walking up the wide streets look-ing for street signs. I had been traveling for two months since the writers' conference—having looped around the country once, about to begin a second pass—and was low on funds, sick with a head cold, exhausted.

When I finally asked a group of young men and women where such and such a street was, it turned out they lived on it. Turned out, small world, that one of them knew my friend. So I started walking with this group of young hippie grunge heads, who took me to a café somewhere in the Haight where all their buddies were in the middle of a tribal council around a big, pockmarked table. There were calls for me to sit down, faces leaning in asking about my old friend. People were fighting to buy me coffee, passing me hand-rolled cigarettes.

When I looked around and saw all those young, earnest faces— smiling ones next to sad—I wanted to burst into tears, wanted to hug every one of those skinny bodies and get down on the floor and roll in all that café dirt, laughing and crying for the wild freedom racing in my veins. I didn't know a soul, was fresh into a strange city, and already I had been let into a circle of friends, treated like some honorary guest. I was truly a lucky man! Thankful for all the attention and kindness, thoroughly overwhelmed, I wondered where the magical ride of *Now* would take me next. I was so hungry I was about to pass out. Talk turned to a show somewhere nearby, then to some girl whom everyone seemed to be in love with, who already sounded like a posterized myth. Sitting back and taking it all in, I was acutely aware of a young woman's shoulder against mine, her warm fingers pausing on my wrist as she bummed a light from my cigarette, leaning in all patchouli and sweat.

After that first café, I half remember searching out a bar with a pool table, downing beer after beer, then heading into another bar that served cheap vodka for a buck a shot and had old polkas on the jukebox. The basic barhopping scene. I spent at least an hour arguing with a drunk about who wrote truer poetry, Dylan or Rimbaud, not even sure we were talking about the same people. Stumbling back to someone's apartment, crashing on the floor, waking up in the middle of the night, throwing up in the toilet, hunched over in the dark in that familiar cold sweat, keeping my numb attention on the old copy of *Fear of Flying* in the corner.

I sleepwalked through a week of this, too lazy or apathetic to pick up and continue on my way. Until the night I returned to the apartment to find all the housemates gathered around the kitchen table. The way they stopped when I walked in tipped me off that they were talking about me. I sat down to stony silence, and their communal posture of passive-aggressive hostility started to flash a bright, easy-to-read GO. It was one of those no-brainer epiphanies where you smack your head with your fist. I didn't really know or like these people, nor they me. I certainly didn't trust them. And in the same coming-out-from-under-the-anesthesia moment, I went up to the spare room and stood in front of its huge garage-sale mirror. What I saw frightened me. I looked like those eighteen-year-old kids downstairs who acted and looked like hippies but weren't. I looked like a dead-tired, underfed, strung-out young man tripping over his own momentum.

I remember going out to clear my head, and the way the street-lights made little pools of light for me to walk through. Remember calling my brother collect, and when he answered after at least a dozen rings, how I nearly cried I was so happy to hear his voice. He asked me why I wasn't in Seattle yet; he was throwing a big party and wanted me there.

"In your honor," he said, excitement in his voice. "People here who want to meet you."

It had been almost two years since I had last seen my brother. Hearing his voice, I realized just how much I missed him. More than anyone else, he knew me. Knew my fuckups and forgave them in advance. By the time I got off the phone, I was about jumping out of my skin. I headed back to that apartment, grabbed my things, and walked out to the corner Wash & Spin. I had eighty dollars in cash, close to a hundred in traveler's checks. That was all. Some street guy was talking in my ear about Jehovah being a conservative. He lifted up his prayer-laced hands toward the ceiling and hummed in a private chant. When the clothes were clean and folded, I wished the guy luck and gave him a freshly minted dollar bill. He bowed down in front of the change dispenser and chanted at me happily, and I went back to the house with one of his spontaneous run-on Beat poems in my shirt pocket.

Early the next morning, I showered and shaved, then grabbed a breakfast of granola and water. I left some money on the table and wrote a quick thank-you note under the Jehovah guy's poem. I was halfway out the door when one of the roommates called after me. His hair was standing straight up, and he was rubbing his exposed belly.

"Hey, man!" he said. "Wait up!"

I was afraid he was going to accuse me of something, demand more money.

"Hey, man, thanks for the bread. Say hey to your buddy when you see him."

Then he gave me a quick soul hug, which only made me feel guilty for trying to sneak out, for a whole bunch of things I couldn't—and anyway didn't want to—articulate.

WHAT WAS SUPPOSED to be a couple of weeks in Seattle dragged on for a ragged, dissipating year. For the first few months I lived in Bill's basement. To make money, I worked the midnight shift at a bakery bagging and delivering bread. When my hours got cut back, I started delivering pizzas on weekend nights. I'd light a big joint when I got off shift, blast Billie Holiday in my room, and masturbate into my pillow.

Bill was happy in his life. He was painting a lot and working at a local music store where he was teaching African drum classes. I don't think his girlfriend, Rochelle, was very happy having me around. She had two daughters, aged five and three, and needed Bill to help around the house. I kept pulling him away—to shoot baskets, to get stoned with me out in the alley, to catch a movie at the Guild 45th. Rochelle knew how much it meant for Bill to have me in town, so she didn't say anything. Still, she probably wanted me to get my own place.

I don't blame her. I did the dishes, took out the trash, and helped with getting the kids off to school as a form of placation, but it wasn't enough. Deep down, I resented her for having Bill's full attention. It was easy to see Bill took joy in being a partner and a stand-in parent. He loved being that responsible. I know he resented Dad for having been so wrapped up in his own life; this was probably his way of combating its effects. He wasn't going to let solipsism get in the way of his being a strong father figure.

Eventually I got my own place, a studio apartment up on Capitol Hill with a noisy radiator and a view of the dumpster. I worked at a café up on Fifteenth, the opening shift, which left me with afternoons to write. I had found a cheap used typewriter at one of the thrifts down on Union, and put it on a yard-sale table facing the one window. A few poems dripped out, but mostly I crouched in front of a cup of tea and daydreamed of being a great writer.

I started seeing a woman I met on a phone solicitation job, but the same old sex stuff kept coming up, and it wasn't long before we were both tired of it. I'd go over to her place, we'd start making out to Van Morrison's *Astral Weeks*, she'd get hot, and then something would happen and I'd disconnect. It took us an hour or two to talk it all through. She'd wind up sucking me off, or I'd almost break my wrist getting her off with my fingers. Definitely not worth it. When I told her that I had to stop seeing her, she stole my Morrison tape and left a series of nasty notes in my mailbox. The last note consisted solely of the inevitable, electric "Fuck You!"

After several months of relative calm and an unexpected bout of domestic happiness, I got restless and started applying to master of fine arts programs. I had a half-formed idea of getting serious about my writing and so worked nonstop for a month struggling to produce something decent. I came up with a thinly disguised auto-biographical piece about a drunken walk in the woods with my childhood friend. I was living with my new girlfriend in a one-bedroom apartment in Queen Anne, chipping in for rent here and there. When the University of Michigan offered me a partial scholarship, I jumped.

This was around the start of the Gulf War, with everyone saying that Bush Senior was going to send troops over to Iraq. I didn't think much of it—couldn't believe we'd be stupid enough to get into another Vietnam. Just going about my sad-sack days. Then one evening I stepped out for a breather only to find the streets crammed with people. I wasn't sure what was going on, thinking maybe some kind of street fair was down on Broadway. But as I got closer, the crowd became a mass of shouting protesters. I asked a man on the corner if he knew anything. He looked as though he thought I came from another planet. "We declared war against Iraq, you idiot!" he shouted. "Bush has gone and done it!"

I walked on, trying and failing to process this new information. A serious-faced man was passing out flyers. A handbill calling for violent revolution, denouncing the Gulf War. A few hundred yards down the block, another flyer got pressed in my hand, this one advertising cheap jeans. Two, maybe three thousand people had gathered at the community college green. There was a speaker, but the sound was so terrible I couldn't make out what was being said. Didn't really matter. The cameras were there and the people out in force. Not that anyone wanted to act, to march or rise up; no, we all wanted something to happen. And, in a few minutes, it did. The man up at the mike broke a string on his guitar and tried quickly to put a new one on. It didn't work. He tried to string another one. Finally, he threw down his guitar and belted out the tune a cappella. The docile demonstrators woke up and roared their approval.

I broke free of the crowd and walked up a grassy hill in between a couple of sickly trees. The moon was out, a vivid orange, hovering over the brick buildings. In a few steps I had moved away from the crowd: just the moon, the trees, and the cold night air passing into my coat. A Broadway bus lumbered up the hill, sparks from its electrical track flashing in the sky. It stopped to let out another load of protesters, shoppers.

Cyrano de Bergerac was playing across the street at the Egyptian. It was one of those old, revamped houses with lots of curtains and fancy latticework. I crossed the street and entered. I felt like I was avoiding some strange disaster, that I had gone AWOL. I was lost in the dark and would stay there until the danger passed. By the time I stumbled to my seat, kicking over somebody's abandoned popcorn, the movie had already started.

War was being waged on the screen. Cyrano was being held back from the fighting by the beautiful Roxane. The truth was about to come out, Cyrano's true romantic nature revealed. But something in Cyrano—his romantic nature maybe—forced him to resist. He left Roxane and joined his men at the front line. He fought as if to die, side by side with Roxane's true love, but failed by living. He was left alive, wrongly loved. His nose was still huge and his pride unflagging. Roxane fell on her dead love's chest.

I was too wrapped up in the melodrama of my rudderless life to concentrate on the film. Outside, the protesters' cheers and shouts rose in pitch, combining with the shouts of men fighting and dying on the screen. In a few days, I would leave Seattle with the five hundred dollars I got from selling the old Zephyr. I would say good-bye to my brother, leave my girlfriend at the bus station with a bundle of promises and a month's worth of back rent. (Things between us had been heating up, which meant it was time for me to leave.) I would tell her I had to get serious about my writing, with my life, and I'd promise I'd come back during the school breaks, that I'd be faithful. As I boarded the bus, my whole body would start to itch with that old on-the-road rash. And I would have convinced myself that I was setting out on a hero's journey.

The Same Old Leaf

Of course it's all
pell-mell, head over heels, snickers and grief,
love notes and libel, fire and ice. In short:

promiscuous.

WILLIAM MATTHEWS, "Promiscuous"

I ARRIVED IN Ann Arbor broke, lost in the wild thicket of my twenties. The town seemed intensely alive, bustling with students and chock-full of restaurants and cafés, good bookstores and downtown movie theaters. The fall air was crisp, the cars shiny and expensive, the handsome campus stretching out before me like a pleasure garden. Football season was already under way, and though not a big fan, I couldn't help getting caught up in the growing excitement surrounding Big Ten football.

On football Saturday in Ann Arbor you can run naked through the streets and hardly a blue jay will notice. Early in the semester, I was walking home from class and passed down a stretch of railroad tracks, coming out near the Intramural Sports building. Before I knew it, I was moving into a corridor of marching-band cacophony: a small flute brigade perched on the baseball stands knocking out signature lines; four timpani drummers in a row, drumming in perfect sync; and a half dozen snare drummers facing out from the building rattling out staccato bursts. My life had its very own sound track!

Within a week I landed a job at Shaman Drum Bookshop, a hip independent store battling the Border's across the street, and rented a small studio apartment in the grad school ghetto. But right away, things started to go poorly. The short story I was working on for workshop was both horrible and utterly unfixable. I was already drowning in the competitive waters of the graduate-level writing program and fumbling my way through a stint as a teacher's assistant.

It didn't help that I antagonized my cohort by getting drunk and fooling around with as many young women as I could sweet-talk into bed. On a weekly basis, I'd wind up drunk under some young woman's window, throwing pebbles and whispering desperate seduction. The whole thing bottomed out the weekend I slept with one of my fellow M.F.A.'s, who happened to be friends with another poet I had French-kissed the night before. By next workshop the word on me had spread. But instead of wising (or sobering) up, I simply moved on to different scenes, younger women.

Then I started dating one of my students. She was in the Fellini–De Sica film class I was grading for. I didn't know her name but knew she was sexy and sad and sitting alone, that she looked like Kathleen Turner in *Body Heat,* only younger. In about three classes she went from sitting across the auditorium to nearly by my side. I noticed that, too.

The next time I saw her she was smoking a cigarette on the sidewalk outside the Michigan Theater. I'd just come out of the matinee showing of Fellini's *La Dolce Vita* and was still wrapped up in its surreal sensuality. She was talking to the professor but keeping one eye on the door. She saw me coming, smiled, and then quickly turned back to the conversation. On cue, I sidled up and bummed a smoke, standing off to the side and assuming my best Marcello Mastroianni pose. She was stunning, tall and long-haired and sensual-mouthed, one of Fellini's own Umbrian angels, and I wasn't sure I had the nerve to speak to her.

After a few minutes, she extracted herself from the ever-growing clutch of young women around the professor, hooked her arm into mine, and deftly maneuvered me away from the other students. "Wasn't that scene in the fountain romantic?" she whispered. I had been rediscovered.

We talked furiously, our hands at our eyes to block the dazzle of the late afternoon light, basking in the Romeo-and-Juliet glow of mutual attraction, and when a rain-soaked breeze came in and picked up the awnings along the street, we took refuge under the theater's massive, old-fashioned marquee. The sudden downpour had the pavement dancing at our feet.

I wouldn't let her leave until she agreed to see me again. *Don't worry*, her laugh indicated, *I'm interested.* When she stepped off the curb, her hand angled over her head to block the rain, she looked like a Balinese dancer.

That night, my girlfriend from Seattle called, wanting to know if I had met anyone. The accuracy of her radar was spooky.

"No, I haven't met anyone," I said, watching myself in the mirror.

"But if you do, you're going to tell me, right?"

I told her I would, surprised at how easily the lie came.

My new friend, Carolyn, met me for coffee the next day. She arrived late, striding up, her head cocked to the side, a big mouth smile blooming on her face. In her hand was the paper she had written on De Sica's *Umberto D.* I remembered it for its suggestive reference to a pepper grinder rubbing up against a woman's pubis.

That and the A I had so enthusiastically scribbled on the page. We laughed at our predicament.

Later, on a walk through alleys and across lawns, our bodies fell naturally into step. I told her I had the eerie feeling that we had been childhood sweethearts, knowing as I said it how much closer she was to her own childhood than I was to mine.

"Of course we were, silly."

At a street corner somewhere on the outskirts of town, she leaned over. "I am," she told me, "only nineteen."

I said something dumb like, "Okay by me." She was in a relationship, she informed me, thinking of ending it.

"Me, too," I said, though it was the first time the thought had entered my mind.

We ended up embracing on my ship's bunk of a bed, hands intertwined in each other's hair. The fact that I was becoming intimate with one of my students did not seem questionable behavior. I simply turned over her next essay to the professor and called my now ex-girlfriend in Seattle. I told her everything.

"You wanted to know," I reminded her. A bitter laugh floated into my ear.

This is it, I told myself, *I am going to start over.* She asked me to reconsider, to slow down, but Carolyn was already naked in my tub, thumbing through my dog-eared copy of Kundera's *Book of Laughter and Forgetting.* I had gone too far to turn back.

I RATIONALIZED THE whole thing by telling myself (and anyone who'd listen) that I wasn't a real teacher, that the professor could grade her papers. Carolyn and I simply ignored the stares around campus and frequented the bars known for not carding young coeds. We spent most nights hanging out in Carolyn's apartment, watching movies with her roommates, sleeping on her floor-bound futon. It was a fun, sexy, heady time, and Carolyn and I convinced ourselves we were head over heels in love.

At least, that's what it looked like on the surface. Deep down, I was scared. Scared that I couldn't hack it in my workshop, that I was too skinny and maybe even had AIDS. (I obsessed about it for months, then finally went and got tested.) I was worried that Carolyn would leave me, and I'd be left alone. I was close to losing my job at the bookstore, credit card bills were running up, and I was barely keeping up in workshop. I'd come home from a shift at the bookstore and wait for Carolyn outside her class. I'd light a cigarette and stand in the hall, trembling.

When the year ended, Carolyn jetted off to experience the junior-year-abroad thing in Europe. It was a godsend, really, for the relationship had begun to die, mainly due to my persistent and embarrassing inability to maintain an erection. Most nights I couldn't have coaxed the thing awake with a cattle prod. Then I started getting long letters from Europe in which Carolyn both promised she still loved me and informed me that she was leaving me. I kicked myself for letting her get away. I even tried to convince myself that I'd change, that the whole impotence thing was some weird, inexplicable phase I'd miraculously move out of.

Soon after Carolyn left, I ditched the overpriced studio apartment and retreated to the convalescence of a university co-op. I'd been laid off at the bookstore after a string of bonehead moves and was desperate. I needed to be around people, have food easily available, specific tasks to perform. Though I didn't see it at the time, and wouldn't have admitted it if I did, I needed help.

Help arrived in the form of Ali. I first spotted her as she stepped out for a smoke after one of our co-op potlucks. She seemed lonely and a little lost. What got me was the warm, open look in her eyes. (Once you've slipped into predator mode, it's hard to step out of it.) I knocked on her door the next night, drawn out of my room by the Dylan she was blasting from her stereo. "Shelter from the Storm," as I remember it. She smiled as if she had been hoping I'd come by and let me in without a word.

We spent the beginning of fall semester getting to know each other. Ali had just started a Ph.D. program in social work. She had ended a short-lived fling with an older guy at the end of the summer before coming out here from Massachusetts. She told me how sex for her had often been stressful; for the first time the sex was hot and fun, but the rest of the relationship was lacking. It didn't help that in high school she had been forced to do some things she didn't want to do sexually, or that she had juvenile rheumatoid arthritis in her hips and other joints that forced her to take anti-inflammatory medications, or that, when in a flare-up, her mobility was limited for days, or even weeks, at a time.

All this to say: she wasn't interested in leaping into bed with a new boyfriend. And when I told Ali about Carolyn, about my struggles with impotence, she actually seemed cool with it. I'd lucked out. For the first time in my dating life, the issue was set aside, not condescendingly or maliciously—or worse, with false compassion—but lightly, in a goofy, grand gesture of good spirits. She didn't want anything to spoil our fun.

We played a lot of Frisbee those first few months, stayed up late laughing and making tapes, drinking wine and smoking too many cigarettes. We talked a lot about our growing attraction to each other, but for a while at least managed to avoid doing anything about it.

At some point in the flirtation, we started telling each other about our families. I gave Ali all my stock stories. I tried to convince her that I actually liked moving back and forth between my divorced parents—that I was able to see the country, meet all kinds of people. To impress her with my bohemian past and gain her sympathy, I told her tales about my "famous poet" father and his string of women. Of our wild bachelor days in Seattle. In each, I portrayed myself as the underdog—the sensitive son left alone for hours, the younger brother under his older brother's thumb. And when I ran out of those, I related how my hippie stepfather helped bring together a utopian commune in the New Hampshire woods. I had told them all so many times I'd lost track of why exactly I was telling them. They'd become part of my con.

I knew I really liked Ali the night she told me about her father. We were out at a café drinking too much coffee, and she had been telling me about how, when she was a small girl, her dad would carry her around the house and show her all the photographs on the walls. He called it the "walk-around." When they got to the upstairs hall, which was lined with family photos, he'd ask: *Who's that?* She'd answer: *That's Grandpa.* Or: *That's you, Daddy.* He'd stroke her hair, then move on to the next photo. He'd say: *Point to Mommy. Point to Ali.* And she would, until she was sleepy enough to go down for her nap. And she told me about the funny stories her parents used to tell her, the nicknames her mom came up with for everyone. The little songs they'd sing.

I remember watching Ali's face as she recounted these memories. Her eyes were wide with happiness and her hands kept rising up out of her lap to describe imaginary shapes in the smoky café air. It was a little like seeing her as a kid—she obviously loved her parents—but there was more to it than that. Every now and then, she'd stop and look at me, making sure I was following her. I would nod my head and tell her to keep going. When she started talking again, I saw that she was describing what she valued in a person— warmth, caring, humor. She was introducing me to her heart.

"I can see you being that kind of father," she said later as we walked back along State Street.

"I hope so," I said, taken aback and, for the moment, unworried about the implications of what she'd just said.

"You will. I know it."

Ali and I were still dancing around loving each other then— one step forward, two steps back. Her friends wondered what she saw in me. They knew about Carolyn, and probably about the impotence. It was an easy call. *Dump the sorry asshole.* But, despite everything, Ali believed in me. She wasn't stupid, or more naïve than the average twenty-two-year-old. She saw something in me, *heard* something in me. So she listened to it—not to her friends, not to me, even when I started talking about Carolyn.

AS THE SEMESTER, and our friendship, unfolded, we found ourselves more and more frequently in each other's arms about to kiss. One night in the co-op game room, after a pitcher of margaritas, Ali and I ended up half undressed on top of the pool table. It started out as our typical line-crossing flirtation, with its requisite polite kisses and pull-aways, but then quickly escalated into something more truly passionate. When I started taking off Ali's overalls, I was shocked out of our drunken play. We lay there, panting, looking into each other's eyes. It wasn't so much that we were heading into lovemaking that brought me up short. We had seen it coming. No, it was the intensity of the passion.

Though we stopped ourselves from going any further that night, clearly things had changed. After that, our flirtations escalated: we kept drawing lines we agreed we definitely shouldn't step over, then, in a flush of passion, we'd jump across. For weeks, making out was okay but nothing further, then we graduated to taking off each other's shirts. Things came to a head when we went Up North to Ali's cousin's lake house near Traverse City. Ali and I had been introduced as a couple, and so we were given a room to share. That night, after dinner and a chilly walk along the shore of Crystal Lake, we jumped under the covers in the queen-size bed. I wanted to make love but Ali wanted to talk. Frustrated but trying not to show it, I could tell that Ali was fragile. I asked her what was on her mind.

"Why do you still want to be with Carolyn after all the humiliation she put you through?"

"Hey, she didn't put me through it. It's me who couldn't get it up, remember?"

Ali sat up, angry.

"You *can* make love, Sebastian. Don't you know that? And you do, you make beautiful love to me. It's fucking you have a hard time with."

"Not-so-hard time with, you mean."

"Oh, come on, Sebastian. Don't you see there's more in this world than your dick?!"

We went on like that for a while, arguing over what exactly constituted lovemaking. For me, fucking *was* lovemaking. Ali disagreed. She thought the intimacy we had already shared—the kissing, the touching—was lovemaking. Finally, out of sheer frustration, I told her that I didn't need to have sex. That I'd rub her back. That we'd just kiss and cuddle. I did it as a kind of concession, feeling like I had failed. But Ali seemed relieved, happy almost. As we were drifting off to sleep, she whispered, "Thank you."

Ali woke in the middle of the night, and as she lay there looking up at the moon through the skylight, she was overcome with a feeling of calm. She realized that everything between us was okay, that we'd be all right. She woke me up to tell me this and, half asleep, I took her in my arms and held her until she drifted off.

In the morning, we went out to breakfast. I was feeling happy, assured by our late night intimacy, but then Ali started crying and I was back to being confused. I thought we had worked things out; that I was doing what it took to be with Ali. But Ali kept crying. She cried through our pancakes. She cried through refills of our coffee. Cried as I paid the bill and cried on the drive back to the lake.

"I can't do this anymore," was all she could say. "I just can't."

"Ali, don't cry. You said it yourself, this will all work out."

"This sucks!"

"What are you talking about? What about last night?"

She stopped crying and looked at me. She was angry.

"If this is what's supposed to happen, why are you still with Carolyn?"

On the drive back to Ann Arbor, I was ransacked with conflicting emotions. I was frustrated beyond belief. I was ashamed. I wanted to go and fuck someone else. (Maybe the cute undergrad who had been flirting with me at the bookstore. She seemed interested enough.) More than anything, I wanted to pack up and leave town—maybe head back to Seattle, see if my old girlfriend would take me back.

The next night I knocked on Ali's door. We talked and talked and then lay down in bed. I was hard, and Ali seemed excited, so I started to make love to her. But when Ali wanted to change our position, I resisted. I had just found a rhythm and wanted to make sure I didn't lose my hard-on. Ali froze up. I asked her what was wrong.

"You can only go at lovemaking one way."

"That's not fair."

"When you're rigid like that it shuts me down," she said. "It just makes me disconnect from myself."

I argued with her about it but knew she was right. I *did* need to do it a certain way. If she moved too much at the start, or needed me to shift my weight, I'd get scared that I was going to lose it. I'd force her back. And that wasn't cool. But it felt to me worse to accommodate her need and then end up wilted and embarrassed. I needed to focus on what worked, didn't I?

"Oh, whatever! Fucking's not the be-all and end-all."

"Oh yeah?"

I threw Ali down on the bed and devoured her in a mock-passionate embrace. She writhed under me, pretending to be in the throes of an orgasm. It was funny, so we kept it up until real passion flared up between us. I was hard again, and eager to show her that I could use it. Ali seemed scared, but she took hold of me and guided me between her legs. I wasn't inside her more than a few moments before she asked me to stop.

"You're being too rough. Slow down. Here, come lie down. Let's take it slow."

I wanted to keep going, but she insisted we stop. We ended up going to sleep frustrated with each other, backs turned.

I KEPT MY distance for the next few weeks. Ali had asked me to. I'd made a few friends from the M.F.A. crowd—mostly guys, fiction writers, who didn't care too much that I had made a fool of myself the year before. We played pickup basketball on the local courts and went to bars afterward to talk literature and watch sports on TV. This was the first year of the Fab Five, Michigan basketball's all-freshmen starting squad, who were well on their way to the NCAA finals. We sat in the bleachers to watch Chris Webber and Jalen Rose dismantle their rivals, Ohio State. There was something truly enthralling about watching those five young hotshots in their super-baggy shorts and black socks as they run-and-gunned their way past their startled opponents.

My father came out to give a reading, but I only saw him for a few minutes at the bookstore party. Pat had stayed behind in Manhattan. I brought Ali, even though we weren't officially dating, and introduced her to my father. She was eager to meet him. But my father didn't seem to even register her presence. I tried to explain to Ali why he might have acted like that. I couldn't, though not because I didn't know why. I think I knew. He didn't stop to meet her because he wasn't sure I'd be with her very long. It pissed me off that he'd do that to her—to me!—especially after all the times he had expected me to accept the strange woman at the breakfast table. But it didn't surprise me.

Ali and I talked about just being friends, and agreed that maybe we had met at the wrong time. There was no reason to ruin a true friendship for the sake of a few nights in bed. Ali urged me to appreciate the things we could share. We might start, she suggested, by leaving each other alone for a while. It sounded smart, but it felt all wrong. I was confused. I had such strong feelings for Ali but didn't know what to do about the sex thing. Though I was ready to end it with Carolyn, I wasn't sure I could actually go through with the breakup, especially long-distance. Carolyn and I had a few tortured phone calls. She knew about Ali and me, and was unabashed in sharing with me descriptions of the various men she was meeting. We agreed things weren't working out for us, but neither of us could bring ourselves to officially call it quits.

A few weeks after our trip north to the lake house, Bill Clinton was elected president. Ali had gone to a party at her cousin Ellen's house over in Burns Park and come back tipsy from the wine and light-headed over the election results. She showed up at my door glowing—"despite myself," she told me later—and we danced and drank together in my room, blasting Joni and Dylan and Indigo Girls. That night was a turning point for us. The hopeful spirit of the election spilled into our hearts; we felt renewed, lifted by elation. For once, our timing seemed right. If we were just friends, at least we were good friends who were sharing a rich and rewarding life.

And as we danced around that room full of books and records and dirty clothes, I caught a glimpse of the future. In it Ali and I were together, happy, dancing to music in a house that we shared.

"This is good," Ali said.

"Yes, it is," I agreed.

"This could be *really* good," Ali said.

We stopped in the middle of the room and looked at each other. We both knew what the "really" was pointing to, but we didn't care. We were too happy to come to terms with the complexities it suggested and so kept dancing.

It took a series of emotionally fraught, dovetailing conversations to shake things up, but finally it was clear that I had to decide, once and for all, between Ali and Carolyn. We both knew what we had was special, beyond "just friends," and Ali had been waiting around in dating limbo for too long. I knew she was right, but I wanted to make the decision on my own. I knew I was good at starting things, at dreaming and passion and flirting, and that I was not so good at following through. Intimacy scared the hell out of me.

AT THIS TIME I came up with the idea for the road trip. I was writing another story about my childhood in workshop, and it had gotten me thinking about my parents' divorce. Through a series of long talks with Ali, I decided that I needed to confront my parents about it, ask them some questions. Not surprisingly, Ali was all for the idea. The social worker in her came out when she advised me to interview them. We spent a whole afternoon writing down possible questions on a legal pad.

So, in keeping with the misguided grandiosity that fueled me then, I decided I could break up with Carolyn and confront my parents about the divorce *at the same time*. Ali would be driving east to visit her family for the winter holidays. I would ride with her to New York, then spend time with my dad before officially ending things with Carolyn, who would have returned home to stay with her folks in Westchester County.

I explained the merits of my plan as Ali and I sat on the co-op's patio and drank apple cider.

"I'll confront Dad about the divorce," I said confidently. "Ask him about the infidelities, get his side of the story, you know."

"What makes you think he'll tell you anything now? He's never come clean before."

I wasn't listening.

"Then I'll take the train to Boston and visit Mom and Charter. Yeah, and then I can ask *her* why she left us with my dad, why the marriage fell apart in the first place."

Ali was frowning now.

"You might think of some other way to put it, don't you think?"

"Then you come and get me, meet Mom and Charter, and we'll head back to Ann Arbor for the new semester."

Ali had had enough. She took a last sip and stood up.

"A neat plan, in theory."

She was halfway inside the co-op before I realized she was leaving.

"And breaking up with Carolyn will free me up to be with you," I called after her.

She stopped for a second and smiled. "As long as you're not alone, right?"

Then she was gone, pulling the sliding glass door shut behind her. I couldn't remember why I was going back to confront my parents, unsure as to what exactly I'd ask them, or what I might gain from hearing their answers. Was I, once again, turning over the same old leaf?

Refuge of the Road

Love might ask anything of you.
Or fire might ask anything of you
and say that its name is love.

WILLIAM MATTHEWS, "A Late Movie"

WHEN I THINK back on that ill-advised trip, I see Ali and me as two characters in a bad road movie. It's easy to picture us heading west on Interstate 90 late on a bright, cold winter morning. Ali is behind the wheel, drawing off her Camel Light; I'm staring out the passenger window, a look of frustration set on my mouth. We've taken Route 125 to Interstate 495 to 290 and are traveling seventy miles per hour in the center lane. Renegade semis pass us on both sides. A couple of hours out of Boston, on our way back to Ann Arbor after a long holiday break: no words have passed between us since we first got in the car, and the strain from the charged silence we've been maintaining so steadfastly is beginning to show.

Another hour slips by. I take over at the wheel. The only words we share are functional: *Enough heat? Could you change the tape? I need to pee.* Ali's face is drawn from a bad night of sleep; when she nods off, her head tilts over to the frosted windowpane and her breathing gets heavy. "You're tired," I tell her sleeping form. When

I look in the rearview mirror, I notice large circles under my eyes and think, *This indecision thing sucks.*

In Manhattan, when we tried turning onto my father's street, a moving van was blocking traffic. Men were stepping out of cars to watch the van thread its way through a hole a few inches wider than its load. While we waited for the traffic to decongest, I took the opportunity to explain.

"You know I am not *in love* with Carolyn anymore, don't you?"

Ali steadfastly ignored me.

"I need to see her one more time to make sure there is nothing left. I have to have some kind of closure."

I knew I was being a jerk. But it had been five months since I had seen Carolyn. The truth was (and I believed Ali knew this) I wanted to make love to Carolyn, wanted to prove, once and for all, that I was a capable lover. Maybe I could make up for months of unrewarding sex in one glorious night. And then walk away from it, redeemed.

Ali gazed out her window as an old woman and her tiny dog made their way, tree to tree, down the sidewalk.

"We'll see each other in a week," I said. "I'll know better then where I stand. It's the best I can do."

Ali's reply: "I can't wait around for you anymore."

I wanted to say something that would make her smile, but there was nothing to say, and so I watched her watch the old woman watch the dog. Then the truck was free. Cars honking. Ali extended her cheek for a kiss. Then I was out on the street, backpack loose on my shoulders, looking up at the windows of my father's apartment.

·   ·   ·

PAT WAS VISITING her family in Rochester, New York, so it was just me and Dad for the first few days. For dinner he took me out to some Mexican place owned by a local sports celebrity. We returned home to catch a Knicks game on the MSG channel. Starks was on fire, hitting an array of fallback jumpers, and Ewing had his usual twenty-point, ten-rebound night. The game was over in the third. Dad opened a bottle of merlot, and during the time-outs I told him the whole soap opera story of my love life. Dad listened with a distracted, eyes-turned-away concentration, now and again offering a reluctant nod of sympathy. I wasn't being very coherent, but it didn't matter. It was all a prelude, anyway.

After another glass of wine, and in between cuts off Miles' *Tallest Trees*, I took a deep breath and jumped in.

"Dad, what was the divorce like?"

He was sitting with a faraway expression. One arm was thrown back over his head; the other hand was up at his mustache, fussing. He was probably thinking to himself: *Which one?* After a few minutes, he said:

"Your mom wanted to buy a house. At the end of everything, I mean. I think it was a last-ditch effort to save the marriage." He laughed to himself. "She wasn't happy being a faculty wife. Imagine that."

"Why did you split? Wasn't there a way to patch things up?"

Dad looked into his wine, swirling the last sip around. The music had stopped, and we were left with the disparate street sounds outside.

"What can I say? It just happened. The line between us simply went dead. We certainly didn't want to hurt you two."

"Well, guess what, you kind of did."

He got up abruptly and disappeared into the kitchen. I wasn't sure if he was coming back. What was I hoping to get out of this, anyway? That I'd somehow come to terms with my parents' divorce and straighten out my own fucked-up life in one fell swoop? And why did I believe I could ever really confront my father about his affairs? Or think he'd do anything but make an elegant dodge? Why couldn't I get angry with him directly?

He returned with a new bottle of wine and a clean ashtray. I could tell by the way he sucked on his lower lip that he was trying to hide his anger, too.

"Listen, kiddo, you try keeping a family together while teaching a full load *and* getting a literary life off the ground. Things don't always turn out as you plan."

"Yeah, but that's not why the marriage fell apart, is it?"

Dad placed the bottle hard onto the table. For a moment I couldn't read his usually expressive face. Not exactly blank, it was cloudy with mixed emotion. Then he lit another cigarette and leveled one of his withering, professorial stares at me. I put up my hands in surrender.

"I didn't mean that, Dad."

"Oh yes you did," he said.

I stood up. It was my turn to select the music. I picked *Ah Um*, which opens with "Better Git It in Your Soul," a raucous, driving number in which Charlie Mingus spurs on his band with wild exhortations. It shut us both up. I sat back down, letting Booker Ervin's blazing "bebop sermon" do the talking for us.

The irony here: my anger was getting in the way. Neither of us could deal with its unexpected presence, and we were spending all our energy dancing around it, when what we should have done was sit down, face to face, and let it rip. *Dad, I'd say, you ruined your marriage and tore my childhood apart with all your sleeping around. Just admit it.* And he'd nod stoically, and say back, *Son, you're no one to talk. Look at you, you're doing exactly what you're accusing me of doing. Your love life is a mess.*

That's what we should have done, but we didn't. Instead, we let the wine and the music soothe us. Later, when we had simmered down, Dad talked about how difficult it had been after the divorce to pick up and move; how he had accepted the teaching position at Emerson College only because it had been close to us. He didn't say it directly, but he was talking about being lonely. At least, that's what I heard him saying. He had been drifting from job to job, woman to woman, and though I had up to that point told myself the only thing keeping my father in any way anchored was his connection to his sons, I wasn't so sure about it anymore.

I couldn't bring up the affairs again. I just couldn't. Partly because I was scared to, but partly because so much had gone on since then. He had already remarried twice since Sharon. I tried to convince myself that maybe this time, with Pat, he'd change things. And, as it always seemed to, conversation shifted into lighter, less charged subjects. We talked, instead, of basketball and movies, of the great Cincinnati Reds team of the seventies, of the way Bob Dylan would refashion a song in concert, turning a ballad into a reggae anthem and a protest song into a cheesy number from a lounge act. I asked him to tell me again about the time he lit Anita O'Day's cigarette at the Newport Jazz Festival when he was fifteen and how she asked him, "You having a good time?" Or how Jack Kerouac came to one of his faculty parties in Chapel Hill and sat morosely on their couch and drank their wine.

When my father went off to his study to write, I stayed in the living room, surfing the unfamiliar Manhattan cable channels. I got frustrated thinking about everything that had and had not gone on that night. It never seemed more clear that I was dodging long-term commitment, that I was chain-smoking women. Never more clear that, like my father, I couldn't stop. Somewhere around three in the morning, when the talk show host came out naked, I flicked off the television.

THE NEXT DAY I went to figure things out with Carolyn. We agreed to meet at a restaurant down in the Village. The place was long and empty, and the mirrors on the walls made me feel like we were lost in a fun house. Carolyn had dyed her hair blond, or the sun had bleached it. Either way, she looked great. When I kissed her hello, I could feel passion pulsing in my fingers.

"You look good," I said, trying not to stare at her breasts.

"You look tired," she said, moving the sugar bowl out of the way of my restless hands.

By the time the meal arrived, we had agreed to call it off. She had already met somebody else, was entertaining a few offers. The waitress hovered nearby, eavesdropping on our awkwardness. And she really did still love me, Carolyn insisted. "I just don't have it in me to start it all up again."

I almost believed her. I told her about Ali. All she wanted to know was if I could get it up.

After lunch, we walked around Washington Square mingling with the holiday bustle and the usual seedy drug traffic. We held hands. Now that everything was settled, I felt happier, freer, than I had in months.

"I'm writing stories," she told me.

"Not about us, I hope."

A pause.

"Does it matter?"

We loitered like teenagers, caught a movie at Film Forum (one of Eric Rohmer's lethargic beach movies). We ate dinner, then took the subway back to my dad's apartment—he was holed up in his study—for a final consolation fuck, which, of course, went awry one last time.

Carolyn left in the morning. I walked her to the door.

"Let's stay in touch," I started to say, but the words turned sour in my mouth.

"You're going to be all right," she told me.

"Yeah, I know. So are you."

"Yes, I will."

Pat returned that afternoon. At dinner, she asked politely about Carolyn. I told her that it was over, and that I was glad it was over. Dad was in the other room, reading the paper, so Pat moved us onto the couch. Dad put down the paper warily. I told them about Ali, how I was serious about her but scared to commit. Pat was quiet, full of sympathy. I forget what my father said, except that it was consoling. Something along the lines of, *I can relate*. I wonder now if he saw himself in my predicament. I was certainly walking down the same path. Did he feel partly responsible for the way I was behaving? As my father, as my main role model, did he feel as if maybe he had done a bad job?

———≫

ON THE TRAIN from New York to Boston I found a note that Ali had stuffed into my pack. I didn't find it until I pulled out the novel I'd packed for train reading.

> Bash, whatever you choose to do
> in your life, whatever you learn
> on this trip, just know you'll be fine.
> And know that I love you and want you
> in my life. Remember what we share.
> It could be REALLY good!!
>
> Ali

I closed my eyes and let a slide show of Ali flicker on my mind's screen. Ali in her co-op room, sitting cross-legged on her bed under a maroon tapestry. Up North, at the Sleeping Bear Dunes, her long hair whipping in the wind. In her old Jeep Cherokee, a cigarette in hand, the Grateful Dead on the deck. And in all the mental pictures, Ali is smiling that sweet smile I fell in love with.

When we began the long approach into Boston, the conductor came through hollering out his unintelligible itinerary, and the train slowly rattled past the outlying neighborhoods. The houses were crammed back against the highway, fences only partially hiding tawdry scenes of backyard down-keep (tricycle on its side in mud next to buckets of something, a car half apart, and some poor naked line hanging down almost to the ground). Ramshackle hovels morphed into brownstone apartments; brief glimpses of alleys and side streets glimmering in the afternoon sun. Then we passed into the tunnel, a guillotine fell, and everything momentarily plunged into darkness.

I caught the bus out of South Station bound for Dover, New Hampshire. Charter was standing outside the Peter Pan bus station smoking a butt. Snow was falling lightly. When we made it onto the long dirt road to Scruton Pond, coming to the place where tar turned to dirt, Charter reached down and pulled out a beer from a brown paper bag on the floor.

"Grab one if you want."

There were no words to describe how utterly, bone-weary tired I felt. It was good to be back in Charter's presence. I had always counted on him to cut through all my bullshit and just give it to me straight. I was eager to ask him about first meeting Mom and what he thought of my father back when we were moving back and forth between them. But I didn't know how to bring that up. We passed the swamp where the heron lived in the summer. I decided to bring up Ali.

"Hey, Chart, what do you do when you can't choose between your women?"

"Why do you need to choose?"

"No, I'm serious. How do you know if she's the right one?"

"Who's the right one? That girl Carolyn?"

"No, Ali. You haven't met her yet. She's coming to pick me up."

Charter looked over at me with one of his appraising looks. I let him look.

"One thing I learned from college," Charter said, keeping his eyes on the road. "At a certain point you have to put your dick in your pants and decide what you're gonna do in life. There's nothing wrong with trying to get laid, mind you. It's just there comes a time when the whole thing gets . . . the whole damn parade gets boring.

"The really important stuff, the really good stuff, let me tell you, that stuff comes later. It comes in the middle of the night. It comes when you're busy working on something and you look up and realize a whole day's gone by. That's what really counts. Yuh. That's where you'll find the good syrup."

Charter took a pull from his beer and waggled his hand in the air—not at me, really, but at the night around us.

"Now that's not to say a little pussy ain't a good thing."

And then he laughed that big crazy horse-laugh of his, which got me laughing.

Charter broke into his thickest Mainer accent. "No sahr, I ain't sayin' nothin' of the kind."

When we pulled up to the house, my mom was standing on the back porch, a load of wood in her arm, waving at us.

LATER THAT NIGHT, after one of Charter's spaghetti-in-wooden-bowls meals, I steered the talk around to the divorce. Charter had begun pulling old records. *Sweetheart of the Rodeo.* Dylan's *John Wesley Harding.* A Buddy Guy disc. Dishes were washed; there was talk of a late walk down the snow-dusted road. When I told her about breaking up with Carolyn, Mom was appropriately sympathetic. She even managed to hold off awhile before throwing me an *I told you so* look.

"What!?"

"She was barely of legal driving age," she said.

"Don't start, Mom," I warned her, only half seriously.

Then, maybe as a way to get back at her, I shared what my father had said about her being an unhappy faculty wife. She just shook her head.

"That was another woman," she said. "A whole different me. A lifetime ago. A lot of what I was doing was running from my upbringing. Your father helped me put away my debutante dress."

There was some bitterness in her voice, little traces of it around her mouth when she spoke of my father, but not much. That, too, had burned away. Mostly, she thought their marriage was sadly touching, a little silly.

"Your father talked a good liberated game, but he never really wanted me to participate in his world. And he always had his adoring students. I was supposed to play hostess at the parties."

And, later: "There's only so much I could take. When he started sleeping with them, it was time to go. It wasn't going to change, he assured me of that."

But she liked the younger version of herself, the lone woman setting out on her own, kids in tow, bravely searching out a new life. When the divorce came through, she told me, "I got eight thousand dollars and the bed. That's all."

We talked late into the night. Charter mostly sat back and listened. He had never liked talking about the past, but he seemed to tolerate it from us. He waited, instead, sipping off some Scotch.

"Move past it," he told me later as we stood out on the porch and watched the stars. "It should no longer concern you."

And I knew what he meant. I knew it was time to put the past behind me. I knew I had to stop using my parents' divorce as an excuse for my own immaturity. Charter was right: it shouldn't concern me. But it did.

ALI CAME TO pick me up the next morning. I gave her a tour of the property, proudly pointing out the outhouse, the vegetable garden, and the Japanese rock garden Charter had just created. When we came back inside, Mom brought out cheese and crackers and made us tea. We spent a pleasant hour talking. Mom asked Ali about her family, about her studies in school. Ali answered straightforwardly. She came across as smart, friendly, and engaged in life, which were all requirements for passing my mom's girlfriend test. Charter seemed impressed by Ali's easygoing character.

Around lunchtime, Mom and Charter's adopted son, Manny, stopped by to help Charter haul some wood. Manny had been considered "hard to adopt" and appeared on WBZ-TV's "Wednesday's Child" at the age of fourteen, back when Bill and I were in college. Mom and Charter took him in, despite his limited cognitive and emotional capabilities. Though Puerto Rican by birth, and raised on the rough streets of Springfield, Massachusetts, Manny took to the woods as though he had been born and raised here. I always thought of Manny as happy-go-lucky, a little simple, loving and hardworking. It was a pleasant surprise to see that he had grown up into a solid adult who lived on his own, held down a job at a local nursery, and always remembered to pay his parents a visit.

Manny joined us on a walk down to the Isinglass River, telling us about his new girlfriend and his latest trip to the skating rink in Dover. We made the walk back in comfortable silence and, after a casual lunch, Ali and I started getting ready to hit the road. Manny gave Ali a hug and a pat on the head before joining Charter outside, a clear sign that Ali had been accepted into the family. By early afternoon, we were back on the highway, bound for Ann Arbor and our new, uncertain life—Ali asleep among the winter coats.

I drove us out of New Hampshire into Massachusetts, pulling over to stretch outside Pittsfield. Ali didn't wake up until we were back on the highway. She opened her eyes and stared out at the passing scenery.

"That's where I grew up," she said, pointing out the exit for Pittsfield.

I looked over at her, surprised that she was awake.

"Tell me about it."

Her lips pursed up, and she looked over at me suspiciously.

"About what?"

"You as a little girl."

"I've already told you."

"Tell me again."

"What are you looking for, Sebastian? Entertainment?"

"I just want things to be okay," I said.

Ali acted as if I had been joking. She added: "If you're not going to talk about what happened with Carolyn, then what?"

I drove on in silence. Ali pressed her forehead against the window. Then she rolled her head back my way, her eyes large and unblinking.

"How was your visit with your dad?"

I looked back to the road. "Okay, I guess. You know, the same old thing."

"Did you get to ask him about the divorce?"

"Yeah, kind of. We talked about it, but he didn't really say much."

"That's too bad."

"No, it was fine. I mean, I'm glad we talked."

A string of cars passed on the right. I waited for the last one to pass, then shifted lanes. "He didn't admit to anything." I glanced at the speedometer. I was pushing eighty so I eased off.

"Hey, Ali, my mom really liked you," I said, trying to change the subject. "I'm not kidding."

This wasn't the right thing to say, though, or it was the wrong time to say it, because Ali's face closed down and she turned back to the window. I drove on, the ragged snow line on the shoulder making it feel like we were driving through an arctic desert. To keep awake, I popped in a cassette of Joni Mitchell's *Hejira*: the quintessential road album, filled with tales of failed romance, restless wandering, and self-discovery. Just right for the occasion.

We stopped for gas outside Utica. Ali ran in for snacks while I wiped down the windshield and checked the oil. Then we were back on the highway.

In between bites of an energy bar, Ali asked again about Carolyn.

Stalling, I pointed to an exit sign for the town of Rome.

"I've always wanted to see the Colosseum."

"Funny. You're avoiding the question."

I started to tell her how things went down with Carolyn, but Ali stopped me.

"If you're going to tell me now, I want you to be serious about it."

"We broke up," I confessed with a nervous laugh. I was actually quite serious but for some reason couldn't get rid of the stupid smirk on my face.

By late afternoon we were past Syracuse, an hour outside Buffalo, trying to make it over the line into Pennsylvania. The traffic was heavy, construction cropping up every twenty miles or so, so I focused on driving. Ali lost herself in a book. We ended up pulling over an hour after it got dark and checking in at a brightly lit Days Inn. Registering under my last name.

"Is Matthews spelled with one *t* or two?" the woman behind the counter asked.

"Two."

The woman smiled. "Just like in the Bible."

On the way to the room, we passed a ballroom full of square dancers. The old couples in gaudy cowboy outfits swung around the room to the garbled directions of the caller, who stood and shouted into a cut-rate microphone. It was a surreal, strangely disturbing vision. I hoped it wasn't a preview of things to come.

WE HUNCHED IN a booth deep inside Pizza Hut.

"Okay," I said. "Just friends?"

Ali nodded in agreement, but her eyes told another story.

"No, not just friends," she said.

"Not just friends?"

I looked down at my congealing pizza slice, unable to face her appraising stare.

"I *want* to be with you," I told her. "Just it feels like I'm ending one relationship only to start another. How do I know this is any different? How do you know?"

"I know how I feel. Do you?"

I felt five things at once.

Because it was late, and because the place was empty except for us, we kept getting interrupted by the waitress vacuuming under our feet. She wanted to go home to her kids.

Ali took my hand and looked directly into my eyes:

"Just commit one day at a time. I'll do the same. We'll go slow. If hard things come up we'll work them out. We're right for each other. You said so yourself that night up at the lake."

"I did? I must have been delusional."

Ali hit me on the arm.

"I am not asking you to marry me, you jerk! Don't overthink this. Just each day, that's all we need to commit to. Each day as it comes."

I can do that, I thought. *I want to do that.*

Outside, the night air was strangely warm. As we made our way across the parking lot back to the motel, I felt certainty radiating from inside in warm waves. Not only that, but I felt it (and this was the wild part) coming from inside her, too.

Back in the hotel room, we became shy around each other. Every little move seemed loaded with import. Even a hug felt monumental. To break the tension, I turned on HBO to a dumb bank-robbery flick starring Patrick Swayze and Keanu Reeves. Ali was getting ready for bed, so I sat there and watched the tube. It seemed a young FBI agent, disguised as a renegade surfer, had gone undercover to break up a drug ring. The leader of the gang took the agent under his wing, despite a gut feeling that something was not right with his new charge.

Ali joined me and together we watched the inevitable silliness of the two men fighting over the sexy love interest. At the first sex scene, we turned down the sound and fell back into bed. Everything was easy and fun and sexy. The old troubles were nowhere to be found.

"I am happy for us," Ali said.

I put my fingers to her lips.

"Me, too."

And I meant it. Not a trace of sarcasm to be found.

"Just one day at a time," she said.

"Okay, then, just today," I said. I repeated it to myself, trying it on for size, as if it were a mantra.

"Just today."

I wanted to believe it. One day at a time. More than anything I wanted to believe it. I just couldn't picture it.

"What about tomorrow?" I asked, trying to disguise the question as a joke.

"Don't think too much," Ali told me.

Then she rolled over and put her weight on me. I grabbed onto her and rolled us over the other way. I raised up on my arms and smiled at her the way I imagined a perfectly contented man would smile at his partner. I must have looked ridiculous, because Ali started to laugh. She laughed so hard tears formed in her eyes. I threw myself down beside her and began to laugh with her. And we kept laughing until kisses took over.

After Ali fell asleep, I drew a tub and broke into the minibar. I needed to think things through. Drinking the quartet of miniature whiskey bottles lined up on the edge of the tub was like picking off gallery ducks. I had been replaying the last few days in one giant, drunken tape loop. I saw myself in bed with Carolyn, wilting; with Ali in the car, speechless; staying up late with my father, stumbling for the right words. As an antidote, I summoned up the night's success, lingering over our joyous climax with equal parts surprise and pride. *We did it!*

Later that night I woke up with a fierce headache, the kind of migraine I used to get as a kid. My dad would draw me a tub and put on soft music. Sometimes he'd come in and rub my back. Or he'd sit in the other room, reading to himself, until I was done. And so that's what I did that night. I sat in a hot bath—so hot my skin turned red—and instead of pretending my father was outside, I thought of Ali, asleep in bed.

Barking at My Reflection

                    . . . we make

    paths from our digressions, and from
    our paths, stories, and from those,

    our lives. A few details gather
    to these stories, like eager pets,

    but for each of them a hundred
    are misremembered, or erased,

    as if to leave our children room
    for anecdote. And what will they tell?

            WILLIAM MATTHEWS, "Secretive"

WHEN I CAME across an ad in the local paper for a therapist who specialized in child-of-divorce issues, I decided to give it a try. I had nothing to lose. I trusted Ali, and if she thought I needed help, why not give it a shot? I certainly hadn't figured out much of anything on my own.

The therapist's office was at the back of one of those strange, oxymoronic entities so common in today's suburbia—the office park. The reception room was comfortably familiar, with the requisite bland paintings/posters and the piles of *People*, *Sports Illustrated*, and *Car & Driver*. I could have been waiting to talk with a sports medicine doctor or been next in line to have my eyes checked. Only the color-strip pamphlets of Twelve-Step literature in the corner gave the place away.

Classical music played softly from a radio hidden under one of the standard-issue chairs. I expected Brahms-with-bubbles, or Prince-done-up-in-strings, but it was the local college station. (Bach's birthday. A good sign.) Then Chip came out, eating an apple. It wasn't the easy soft-shoe shuffle of the therapist he had perfected, or the perfectly modulated handshake—neither weak nor firm but somehow reassuring. Nor was it the arty photos on the walls of his office or the comfortable sitting chairs facing each other at a reasonable distance. (Though these helped.) It was the bemused look on his face, the tricky glance he shot me from behind his wire-rimmed glasses as we stepped inside. If he hadn't been so genuinely friendly, I'd say it was a cocky look. The kind of look the short point-guard wannabe gives you on the basketball court when he thinks he's got your game down. That's not exactly right, for somehow I was in on the joke.

It took three hour-long sessions to lay out my poor-pitiful-me story in its entirety. Chip copied down the broken-off branches of my family tree onto a huge tablet of paper propped up on an easel. We spent one whole session mapping out the back-and-forths of my childhood. Chip didn't say much; he just took notes and ate his apples. Near the end of the third session, when I cracked a weak joke about my patrilineal ability to dig myself romantic holes in which to fall, Chip stopped me in my verbal tracks.

"You like to do that, don't you?"

"Do what?"

"Put yourself down. Make yourself the butt of your own jokes."

"Somebody's got to do it."

"You know what they'd say at therapy school about that?"

"Nope."

"They'd say you're covering up your emotions."

"You buy that bullshit?"

"Nah."

He laughed openly, the snicker directed not at me but at the "they" to which we had so brazenly been referring. And with that, he wrapped the apple core neatly in a paper towel and dropped it in the wastebasket.

"Two points," he said, sitting back with an easy smile. "But I do think it's interesting *how* you choose to do it."

"Like how?"

"By comparing yourself to your father, for starters."

I pretended to smack my forehead with my palm, as though I were an idiot for not seeing it before.

ALI AND I rented the top two floors of a three-story house in Ann Arbor a block down from the farmers' market. We had graduated from taking things "one day at a time" to thinking in terms of semesters. Eager to get started in our new life, but afraid to jump immediately into the deep end of living together, we asked one of the women from the co-op to room with us. We needed a lifeguard ready with a preserver. It was a beautiful place, blessed with sun, hardwood floors, and a steep, switchbacking staircase. There was even a flat roof onto which we could climb and stare down at the world. We were happy the way young couples often are, not aware of how irritating our happiness was to those around us. Enthralled, we made lists of one another's charms and carried them around like bundles of flowers.

The apartment had three bedrooms, and the initial agreement had been that we'd each have our own room. This was supposed to help us to take things slow; we'd each have our own space and clear boundaries. And it would be easier on our roommate—three friends, not a couple and a third wheel. But after the first two weeks, Ali and I had moved into one room, turning the second bedroom into a study and writing space. We kept disappearing into the bedroom.

Even so, and despite all our efforts and good intentions, Ali and I were struggling, mostly with sex. Ironically, the openness we had shared at the beginning of our relationship, which had allowed us to approach lovemaking relatively easily, had gradually become more of a stumbling block in our new life than a stepping-stone. It's as if we had covertly agreed to become one another's healer, which made for a strange mix of motives and impulses. We seemed to have left the door open for our past demons to waltz in.

Ali's demon happened to be the two-headed monster of depression and arthritis. In most cases of juvenile rheumatoid arthritis, the young adult grows out of the disease. It just falls away. In a few cases, as in Ali's, the person moves into adulthood carrying the extra baggage of the illness. The depression comes, I imagine, as a sort of delayed grief. You didn't get the childhood you wanted (Ali had to give up competitive ice dancing), and now you weren't going to move as freely in the world as the odds had promised. When the shock of the truth wears off, the depression sets in. Only in her early twenties, Ali had been forced by JRA to make middle-aged decisions.

Soon after we settled into our relationship, Ali decided to confront the depression that had haunted her off and on since high school. It seemed to me a strong move. However, whether a symptom of the depression or a side effect of the medication she started taking, her sex drive began to disappear. For my part, my occasions of impotence, though much less severe, continued to persist. It made me wildly insecure. I was afraid of not being enough of a man. In the past there had been the reassurance that came with promiscuity—the contact high of feeling attractive, the heady arousal of flirting. At least I could fall in love with falling in love. And when things fell apart, I could move on to the next. But this serious relationship thing was hard. I kept telling myself that what Ali and I were going through was positive; it just wasn't *feeling* good. I was used to feeling good—or at least pretending to.

We quickly fell into a pattern. I'd want to make love; Ali wouldn't. I'd badger her into coming to bed with promises of rubbing her back. Things would go along okay until my erection wilted. I would lie back and start to touch myself. Fed up, Ali would roll on her side, facing away from me.

"I hate that you have to do that," she'd say.

"It helps me get ready."

"Don't I turn you on?"

I wouldn't know what to say, so I'd roll over and feign sleep. In the morning, I'd apologize for the night before and try to make it up to her by being especially attentive to her needs. (I bought her a lot of flowers.) Looking back, I can see that this reaction to Ali's question, though immature, was actually an improvement on my old mode of behavior. Before therapy, I would have bolted for the door, gone looking for another lover. Now, at least, I was sticking around to try to piece things together again.

As a way to counteract the insecurity and frustration, or at least postpone it by blowing off steam, I took long, restless walks. Ali understood that this was the best I could do, that it was not so much running away as checking out temporarily: I had to leave the house in order to return. She would follow me to the top of the stairs and wish me luck, assuring me I was okay. Though I knew she was right, somehow I couldn't feel it.

I certainly wasn't getting any work done. With large blocks of free time, I should've been writing. But, perversely, I was unable to keep still or pay attention. I couldn't even sit long enough to scribble a page of rough sentences. This distractibility was pervasive. In each small task, at every turn, I was restless, antsy, floating. At every little distraction—the phone ringing, hunger pangs—I would get up from the desk, grab the packet of smoking tobacco, and lace up my walking shoes. I'd kiss Ali at the front door, already distracted, and, after a halfhearted apology, head outside.

MY THERAPY SESSIONS with Chip were in a rut, too. Chip kept wanting me to talk about my parents, but I kept balking. I didn't feel comfortable labeling my father a sex addict or criticizing my mom. For any harsh judgment of them only indicted me in the process. I'd do my best to change the subject. Most often I'd start talking about basketball. My favorite sidetrack involved using the pickup games I was playing in—as my father once defined it, "that particular balance between pattern and improvisation"—as a working metaphor for a well-lived life. Going with the flow vs. forcing the issue.

Chip was a fan of the game, so we would get a little lost in the idea. I had told Chip about the fights I had been recently getting into on the court, how I would argue foul calls with young hotheads—a few of the verbal tirades almost escalating into thrown punches. Chip thought it was a sibling thing. We'd been exploring the relationship between Michael Jordan and Scottie Pippen; how Pippen was like a little brother to Jordan, always deferring to the dominant older brother and, at the same time, complementing him and backing him up. Of course, I identified with Pippen.

"And who does that make your father—Coach Jackson?"

I shrugged. At that point in my life, I had no idea what to think of my father. I had idolized him for so long, romanticized his lifestyle, that it was hard for me to see the real man through all the gauze of child love. Unlike my brother, who seemed lost in his anger toward our father, I refrained from discounting his importance in my adult life. I refused to cut him out.

"Do you think you'd be able to beat your brother one-on-one now? Is that what you're trying to do in those pickup games?"

"Let's drop the basketball metaphor," I said.

"Fine. Want another one?"

"Sure."

"This dog keeps getting lost in a fun house. Every time it comes across a mirror, thinking it's being attacked, the dog barks furiously at its reflection. Eventually, it calms down. But at the next mirror, the dog sees its distorted image and starts barking again."

"Good story," I said sarcastically.

"You're the dog," Chip said. "And until you find a way out of that building, you will keep mistaking your image in the mirror for your father's. And you will keep picking fights you can't win."

A few sessions later, after a long and elaborate discussion of my dad's infidelities, Chip asked about his relationship with Pat.

"What can I say?"

Pat had recently been diagnosed with cancer. At first, the doctors thought she had only a short time to live; now they said she had a decent shot at surviving.

"Do you think your father will make a good caregiver?"

"He'll be horrible at it."

"Why do you say that?"

"I just know."

"I think you're right."

"I know I'm right."

"Do you think your father is depressed?"

I had never thought of it that way.

"Think about it. He's an insomniac, drinks heavily, struggles to stay in long-term relationships. He gets bad headaches. These are all classic symptoms of depression."

And though it sounded right, I couldn't wrap my mind around the idea. My father was too dynamic, too funny, to be depressed. And, besides, this was just the kind of easy diagnosis that he so disdained. Just the word itself, "depressed," would have made his skin crawl. I didn't feel comfortable analyzing my father.

"That would mean I was depressed, too," I said, confused by my own logic.

"Yeah," Chip said. "You're depressed. I'd agree with that."

"Are you supposed to say that? Aren't you worried I'll lose it or something?"

"You can handle it."

As I often did during our sessions, I spent the next block of time thinking things through, fighting back tears.

"You look sad," Chip said.

"I *am* sad."

"Do you know why?"

"No."

"I do," Chip said, almost in a whisper.

"Why?"

"Not telling." He stood up to signal the end of the session.

As I was leaving his office, Chip came to the door and called after me: "It's in his poems, you know."

I had given Chip one of my father's books at the start of my therapy, so I wasn't surprised that he had read some of his poems. When I got home from that session, I pulled out the manuscript of my father's forthcoming book, *Time & Money*, and started reading. And there it was, like a fog lying over many of the poems; I spied my father's unhappiness on every page.

It was there in the last stanza from "Time":

*I think that's what I'd do. I'd soldier through
the fear and fell depressions. I'd call on
what those critics like nicely to call "wit,"
i.e., the compressed force of my rage
and love. I'd invent whatever it took
to get me through or dead, whichever came
first.*

It was also there in the sad question-and-answer at the end of "The Rented House in Maine": "Why did that marriage fail? I know the reasons and count the ways." In "Grief," with its dark snapshot of misery and anger; in the two poems about his father's death and the one about the diagnosis of Pat's cancer. If he wasn't depressed, he sure wrote about it a lot.

But when I returned to Chip with the evidence I had found, he shook his head.

"That's not exactly what I meant," he said. "Sure, there are signs of depression in the book. Your father writes about his life, about his emotional states and his moods. That means that there are also signs of happiness in the poems. And anger. And amusement. And confusion."

"I know that," I said, realizing as I said it that I sounded like a five-year-old. And I *did* know it was wrong to look at the poems to figure out the poet. Knew my father would have hated that idea. But I couldn't help myself.

"I was trying to read the work *not* as his son," I said.

"I am not sure what that means. Maybe you should read them as a fellow poet."

Chip was right, of course, for alongside all the billboard depressions, equally bright neon letters blinked out my father's abundant anger, his bouts with joy, his perpetual irony. (The opening line of "Self Help": "It would be good to feel good about yourself for good.") And, slowly, what at first seemed like out-and-out unhappiness soon started taking on depth and complexity. There was something brave in my father's examination of these trials and tribulations: he was facing things head-on. Cracking jokes about serious matters. By writing about his emotions, he was finding a way to move through them. Wasn't he?

SLOWLY, CHIP WAS convincing me that I had inherited my issues concerning sex from my father—his fear of intimacy, his inability to stick with one partner. I could see what he meant: I had taken on a truly messed-up way of approaching relationships with women. But that was as far as Chip would go.

"At some point, Sebastian, you're going to have to take responsibility for your own actions."

"I think I do," I said.

"Oh, but I think you don't," Chip said.

"How not?"

"You always make yourself out to be the victim. As if you didn't have any choice in the matter. When are you going to start standing by your convictions?"

Once again, I didn't want to talk about it. More than anything, the truth felt disabling. Whenever Ali brought up the subject of our future together, for instance, despite a real and sincere desire to move in that direction, all I really wanted to do was get the hell out of town. We'd talk about it, and on the surface I'd be fine, even excited about the idea of getting married. But then I'd walk away rigid in fear. My father was the one jumping in and out of marriages, not me. So the fear was mine. It emanated from me, belonged to me, pure and simple.

After a few more sessions digging around in my feelings toward my father, Chip came to the conclusion that I needed outside help. He suggested Adult Children of Alcoholics.

"What's that place got to do with me?"

"Your father drinks, right?"

"Yeah."

"And your mother."

"Yeah."

"And your mom's father was an alcoholic?"

"Yup."

"And you said that you—"

"Okay, I get it. But I am not worried about being a drunk."

Chip leaned back. I could see I had exposed myself somehow.

"So what *are* you worried about?" he asked quietly.

"Want the therapy school answer?"

"Sure."

"You want to hear that I hate myself, is that it? That I fucking loathe myself. Especially the part that comes here and throws up all over your floor. Is that what you want to hear?"

"Is it true?"

I laughed.

"Some days."

"Do you think your desire to be attractive to women has anything to do with your father's drinking?"

"You know, Chip, I have no idea."

We sat in silence. Then an idea came to me. I burned with anger just thinking about it.

"I can't live up to my father. I can't do it."

He looked at me for a while, letting me stew.

"You're not your father," he said softly, reaching for an apple.

"Not by a long shot."

I said it before I could stop myself.

Chip raised an eyebrow. He kept it raised as he polished the apple on his sleeve. He took a loud bite and chewed it dramatically. Then he made as if he were shooting a basket.

"And it's good!"

IT WAS RAINING lightly when I stepped off the front stoop of our apartment. Ali and I had been fighting again, so I was heading out walking again. I rolled a Drum cigarette as I walked, pausing a moment to light the ragged end and watch the loose tobacco flare up. At a break in the traffic, I crossed over Main and headed into the Old West Side, taking my first right, then a quick left, passing over the train tracks that carried the early morning trains through town. Turning up the hill on Fountain, I began the long, slow climb to the top of Hunt Park.

As I climbed up through the old Victorian houses, I started running through my greatest-hits tape of self-doubt. Hadn't been looking hard enough for full-time work. Hadn't made any significant advances on my writing. Wasn't sympathetic enough to Ali's chronic pain. Wrapped up in worry, I allowed my thoughts to crowd out the surroundings, to replace them with chatter. Not surprisingly, I was no longer looking: at house, at tree, at slinking cat.

It got so bad that when I came upon a half-burned-down building, I saw it as a physical representation of my inner state, a shambles that mirrored my own. The possibility of renovation seemed futile—an endless task to be undertaken at imminent peril. A second desecrated house a block up—this one left to rot—became a terrible omen. Brown, flattened grass told of things once held together now coming apart. Even the crows up in the trees played a role in this melodrama, calling to each other from adjacent telephone poles, squawking their walkie-talkie static and flapping off as I passed beneath.

By the time I made it to the top of the arrowheaded park, I was ready to turn back for home. *This is no fun.* But, looking out across the park fields, I was stopped by an unexpected, panoramic view of our small city. The downtown's business district spread out before me, next to it the cluster of old university buildings, with the campus clock tower rising high above the trees. Off to the right, the university's famed football stadium was clearly visible, its gigantic oval of metal seats shining in the sun.

There was something sad about the hugeness of the stadium, about looking down on the humdrum afternoon of city life, that got me thinking about the last few months, and about the future. Ali hadn't been caught up in depression for a while, and her arthritis had settled into an uneasy remission. Still, things could always change back. Her hips had been aching recently, stiffening in the early summer rains, and that could mean a flare-up wasn't far behind. And she had years left on her dissertation. How long could I wait for her? How long could we keep trying to make it work? *I've come a long way since my roaming days, haven't I? Am I going in circles?* Even at this on-high vantage, I felt insignificant, lonely, lost.

Instead of heading home, however, I walked over to the old graveyard at the top of the hill. I hadn't paid it much attention before, but today the shaded grounds felt portentous. Slipping the horseshoe-shaped handle back over the pole, I followed the narrow gravel lane along its circuitous path through the gravestones. Eventually, I arrived at the back of the property, everything still except for one sprinkler in its lurching arc over the grass. Then at the back of the grounds I noticed a flat gravestone in the tall grass at the base of a gigantic oak tree. The gravestone of a young man, dead in his early twenties. It read:

remember me
I live in quiet dreams and secret things,
in hidden pockets, softly away

A wave of great sadness washed over me, followed by the eerie feeling of breath leaving my body. My arms hollowed out, and I came to the visceral understanding that I was standing in the graveyard of my life. That I was a dead man. That my life at that moment could be anything or nothing at all.

Directly behind the gravestone lay a path leading down a steep grade out of the official cemetery property; it made perfect sense to head down into the forest below. When I passed over the lip of the hill, I found myself descending into a barren outback. Directly below me lay a rough oval of cleared land: a handful of young trees and ragged bushes scattered in tall grass. There was no birdsong. The entire area seemed injured, as if burned down and only partially grown back. My first thought was of nuclear testing, or an old, rehabilitated town dump. The bushes that grew over a tumbledown stone wall appeared lived in; it was easy to envision homeless men camping inside their scaffolding. There were a few makeshift paths intersecting, trampled grass and weeds that marked the traverse of joggers, mountain bikers, and wandering dogs. It felt like I had come upon a remote crossroads in a strange, inhospitable land. And, at the same time, it felt like coming home.

THE ACOA MEETING convened once a week at a local church just down the road from our old co-op. I went because I knew I had to, because Ali needed me to go. Because, as they say in the group, "My life had become unmanageable." I hated the whole thing: the passivity of the people surrounding me, the thinly veiled Christianity that presided over the meeting, the clichéd advice people gave under the guise of neutral response. What I hated the most, however, were the truths the people spoke—so pathetic, so true, so like me.

Did I find anything in that anonymous circle? Most days I drew a big blank—the emotional equivalent of TV static. But every now and then I would be taken over by a creeping rage. I'd be sitting facing the big windows that overlooked a small grove of trees, and all of a sudden I'd want to hurt someone, to go out there and beat up one of those trees. Gradually, though, I came to see that my parents' divorce was the split at the center of my childhood. That the split was inside me. It didn't matter how many times I told people that I liked moving to a new school each year, or that it helped build character, I was still reacting to my life as a "survivor." (My least favorite of their labels, but maybe the most accurate.) I could see that almost every move in my life had been principally a reaction to a perceived crisis.

It took me months to come to that small understanding, and a few more to believe it. And, even then, I didn't—couldn't—do anything to alter my situation. I was stuck. So I spent a year sitting in that circle, fiercely independent, wrapped in anger and shame, skeptical of all advances or overtures of brotherly spirit. During this time, I graduated from the master's program and landed a job teaching English as a Second Language at a downtown institute. (I was lucky to find teaching work.) Ali was deep into her Ph.D. program. We still had our struggles, but I kept going to therapy. Our life was good, something to be thankful for.

There is nothing about that year—or no particular time—that I can look back on and pinpoint as the event that changed everything. No epiphanies rained down on my head. Something inside me eventually subsided, a compulsion slackened. Going to the ACOA meetings helped. When something or someone got me riled up, I was able to see myself acting out and could back off a little. The buttons were both pushed less often and more easily pulled back out again. I was a little more in control of my own machine. Sometimes I could even perceive the old familial shadow play being acted out backstage. I didn't know how to change it, but at least I was aware of its insidious presence.

Sitting in that circle of sad, kindred spirits helped keep me in Ann Arbor. I was ready to bolt at the hint of crisis. Everywhere I went, it seemed, angry women would stare at me with spurned-lover eyes. I could hear the mean-spirited gossip follow me down the English department halls as in a water-skier's wake. And every day an old familiar voice whispered in my ear: *Get out of town.* Going to that meeting brought me back in to myself. Ali must have been able to hear the voice, too, for she would counterbalance it by encouraging me to take a long walk, but then come back home.

"You're still stuck in it, Bash," she'd tell me. "You're barking at your reflection."

I hated hearing it, but the look of compassion on Ali's face, and the undercurrent of angry frustration flowing underneath it, kept me from losing my cool. I'd go to another meeting if that's what it took. I'd take another walk into the outback.

My teaching job at the local English-as-a-Second-Language institute made the decision to stick around a whole lot easier. I had to commit to staying for at least four months at a time. And working with the returning adult students, who were so eager to learn and conscious of the money they were spending, helped me lift myself out of my own little set of troubles. I was getting paid to teach them how to write, which was not an easy endeavor. I began working overtime on my lesson plans.

And at each juncture, at every potential crossroads, I kept deciding to stay. Why? I'm not exactly sure. I guess I was staying because, for once, it seemed a better alternative than moving on. What did I learn? I learned that I was lucky to have found Ali. That I was tired of going it alone.

Why I'm Staying

> This life,
> it's easy to feel you've been born on the road.
>
> WILLIAM MATTHEWS, "Straight Life"

IT WAS AROUND this time that I began to notice the masons. Each morning on my walk to work, and every afternoon on the way back home, I would watch them as they steadily erected a second spire, redid the stone steps, and laid stone for the entrance of the St. Thomas Catholic Church. There was a consciousness apparent, a certain attention paid to detail, that slowed my walking. Impressed by their excellent work and the minimum of effort and waste they displayed in carrying it out, I found myself stalled on the corner of Kingsley and State, all of a sudden certain that I was observing cloistered monks going about their sacred tasks.

Most construction sites grow up fast and loud and awkward like a teenager and move away just as messily. There is a violence to the brief stay, a scar left behind that takes a long time to heal. But not here: no radio blares, no shouts back and forth. The only signs of industry were the hollowed-out echo of a hammer, the intermittent wail of a buzz saw, the dissonant rattle of four-by-fours falling into a stack. Church life flowed easily around the men and their work, incorporating them, or they it.

The crew consisted of four, sometimes five men. All but one appeared over fifty. They parked their trucks on a side street adjacent to the church entrance, sometimes under the branches of a huge oak, and sat under its impressive shade to drink their coffee and eat their lunches.

The men spoke softly to each other in a language I could not understand. There were days I was certain they were Russian immigrants or Poles, convinced by the strong early morning coffee aroma, too strong to be from 7-Eleven. Other days, I wondered if they might be a family of brothers, moved down from the Upper Peninsula in search of work in the city.

Day after day the same thing. As I became caught in the delicate symmetry of their work, I began to make up stories. The two men at the spire could easily have been father and son. The younger one was clearly the apprentice—bucket bearer, brick passer, pallet loader. The older man, heavily mustached, compact, and strong, received the bricks without a word and laid them in place. They had a language of gesture and glance. These men were alive in their work; they held an inherent faith in their craft, they were good at it and believed that it would get done. It reminded me of Charter.

Sometimes I waved or nodded at the men, but usually I left them alone. They had no time for a freeloader who meandered from desk to classroom to desk. I had time to kill, the saying goes, my hands soft and muscles slackened from a long, laborless winter. It was as though the street between us had turned into an uncrossable river, the land we stood on separated by a long tradition of war. At the day's end, they went home knowing they were that much closer to completion; I often went to sleep in confusion, crossing out most of what I had written in the morning.

One early April morning the men packed up their things and prepared to leave. As if by magic, the church was restored. I couldn't remember how the structure looked before or see any discernible difference between the new stonework and the old. Only the spires were different, and the new roof stood out a common brown, oxidation not yet bringing the metal to that particular jade green of weathered copper.

How I wanted to cross the empty street and join the men in their rough semicircle! To commend them on their efforts, maybe say something about the quality of light or ask about the source of the granite. How I wanted to step into their world. But I continued walking, stopping farther on to watch as the final flagstone was set before the church doors. Then the dust was swept up, neatly and unceremoniously.

Weeks passed before I walked by the church again. On that day, my teaching had gone poorly, and I could tell I would have little energy left to write. I was critical of myself in the steps between work and home, unforgiving of the small progress I had made. I had been thinking about my father. Actually, I was chastising myself for not being farther along in my career. At twenty-eight, my father had already been teaching creative writing full-time at the university level. He had three published books. (Of course, he had also been married and divorced, and had fathered two children. Ali was quick to point out that I was conveniently ignoring that part.) I was beating myself up for teaching at a language institute, not yet finishing a book.

It was a familiar rant, a reel of self-pity and loathing. And I was sick of it. Picturing my dad at his desk, I yelled, "Fuck you!" An old woman pruning her roses in a nearby yard turned around.

"Not you," I said. "My father."

Strangely, this made her smile. She turned back to her roses and I kept walking, unexpectedly lighthearted. That felt good!

"Fuck you! Fuck you! Fuck you! Fuck you!" I chanted to myself, which felt even better. I was on a roll.

"Fuck my brother, the fucking asshole! And fuck every god-damn fucking stuck-up prick who underestimates me, and fuck all the politically correct assholes who look down on me for sleeping around . . . and fuck Ali for wanting me to marry her so fucking much. What does she want from me?! Fuck her!"

When I reached the once familiar juncture, caught up in ranting, I was surprised by the sight of a group of children bursting forth from the open door of a school bus. The sun was behind a wall of clouds; everything was in muted shades of gray and brown. All, that is, except the boys and girls running headlong and glee-fully over the masons' handiwork, trailing colorful coats and book bags, who crossed over the vestibule into the church like a school of tropical fish passing over a reef, disappearing into the darkness for choir practice or classes or prayer.

WHEN I TOLD Chip about the masons, he asked me why I thought they were so different from me, unconvinced there was all that much distance between us.

"You go to work. You construct things. What's the difference?"

I didn't have an answer. Instead, I told him about my blowup on the street corner. I had surprised myself by swearing at Ali for wanting me to marry her.

Chip sat forward and clasped his hands in front of him.

"This is good," he said. "What did you feel like when this was going on?"

"I don't know. Anger, obviously."

"Was any of the anger directed at yourself?"

"No, for once it wasn't."

"Are you sure? You left yourself totally out of the conversation?"

It took a while, but I eventually reconstructed the inner dialogue that had played in my head as I walked away from the masons. It went something like this:

I am not happy. Poor baby!

I have to stop waiting for things to change, for things to be perfect. No shit, Sherlock!

I am a faulty model: there is something totally, quintessentially, irredeemably screwed up about my person. Fuck me!

Chip was laughing. He looked positively gleeful.

"You're enjoying this?"

"Aren't you? You said, 'I am a faulty model.' That's perfect. For good or for bad, that is what you have to offer. That's all. Whatever else is missing will have to come from inside of you."

"But what if I just keep repeating what my father has done? What if I am stuck in his rut? I don't want to always be sleeping around . . . marry and divorce, marry and divorce, my whole life."

"Damn, Sebastian, you don't quit, do you? Why is your father the only suitable model for you? What about your mom and Charter? Or Ali's parents, for that matter? Haven't they been happily married for years?"

"I look to them, too."

"Maybe. But how about looking to yourself first."

I was empty of smart-ass remarks. And, as I often did, I walked away from that session knowing that we had uncovered something important. But it wasn't until I drove home from a weekend pickup game, sore but happy, that I had some insight into the matter. At the start of the next session, I told Chip about the game. Though I hadn't played well, our team had won. I managed to hit the one open jump shot that came my way, and didn't make a fool of myself on defense. More important, I avoided getting into a fight. For once, I hadn't let my temper fly loose into the face of some kid ready to match its force and wrestle it—and me—to the ground. A minor accomplishment in itself.

Chip knew that for the last few months I had been joining my friends on Thursday nights at a local school gymnasium for friendly games of four-on-four. It was he who pointed out that when I started my chip-on-the-shoulder routine, now there would be quick counteraction. He was right. Fourth-grade humor was the most effective tactic. If I got worked up over a dumb call, my friend Luke would pull down my shorts on the fast break. If I held on to the ball too long, David came over and deposited a wet kiss on my forehead. I had kicked the habit in less than a month. It took a while, but eventually I found the subtle balance of playing hard and competitively without letting excessive emotions spill out.

Of course, the real test came on a park court in a real pickup game, where testosterone levels go unchecked and strangers share intimate space. And this time I had passed.

"I hope it's a sign that I am growing up a little," I told Chip.

"Nah," he said, pulling out an apple and smiling. "I think you're regressing."

"I am serious, Chip. I think I'm getting somewhere."

"So do I."

. . .

ALI AND I were still living in our Kerrytown apartment, but talking about finding a new place the following fall. I had begun teaching composition courses at the University of Michigan, and Ali had recently completed her prelims, achieving doctoral candidacy, and was now starting the long, arduous process of writing her dissertation. We had been talking a lot about getting engaged. After more than a year of melodrama, now all of a sudden I wanted more than anything to stay put. Go figure! It helped that spring was in full bloom, and that the outdoor basketball courts were finally clear of snow; that I had classes to teach, meetings to go to, friends to take walks with. I was even taking beginning yoga classes, something I had been saying I was going to do for years. Our lives weren't entirely centered around the university anymore; we were making new friends as a couple, going out to dinner or a movie, then coming back to talk around a fire. It all felt so adult. I never thought I would enjoy living such a *traditional* life.

One afternoon I came home determined to clean the house. We had let the refrigerator get smelly, and the cupboards were conspicuously bare. I would clean the kitchen and go for a shop. I was excited by the rare, open afternoon that lay before me. However, a note on the table altered my plans. Ali had scribbled down a phone message from the teacher of my recently completed meditation course. It read: *The time is NOW to work on the temple while the weather stays warm. Call Sukha.*

It was as if Sukha was commanding me to pay attention, as if she saw me as a lazy good-for-nothing. I had to agree. For I did owe

Sukha twenty dollars for the last course and said I would pay it off with work, having made the promise more than two weeks earlier.

I stood over the note a moment longer. *Of course* a phone message from a Buddhist teacher would say "the time is now." This was no different from the whack on the shoulder for the sleeping initiate. I changed into work clothes and stepped back outside. After a quick drive across town, I parked around the corner from the temple. When I turned the corner, the chalked-out words "this" and "way" passed under my feet, along with an arrow that pointed me toward the temple. I had to laugh, marveling at how easy the universe was moving me along. I was even getting directions.

Sukha answered the door in mild surprise, saying simply, "You came." I smiled and half bowed. Right away, she set me to work scraping, then painting two window frames. I worked for close to two hours, stopping just as the last light slipped from the sky. I washed the brush as mindfully as I could, searched around for a safe place to set the paint can, and folded up the drop cloth.

When I returned home, I took up the household chores, then sat down at my desk to write. Dylan on the turntable. Ali was working on a project at the kitchen table, laying out piles of envelopes and sticking labels on them.

"I think we should get married," I said.

Ali looked up, pleasantly surprised. "Where'd you get that bright idea?"

"I don't know. I read it somewhere."

"Did Chip give you the idea?

"Give me a break. I am just saying I think it might be time."

Ali stood up and took my hands in hers.

"Are you proposing to me?"

"I am not sure."

"You better have a ring if you're going to propose to me."

"Definitely not a proposal."

"Okay, but I'm not going to let you back out of this. You said it."

"I know what I said. Just give me a little time."

First thing, I needed to come up with money for the ring. I asked Ali's cousin Ellen and her husband Marc for a loan. They were happy to help out. Then I took Ali shopping a couple of times, watching nonchalantly as she tried on rings. I went back to the stores later and checked to see if the ones she lingered over were in my limited price range. Finally, I found the perfect ring at one of the antique jewelry stores down on Main Street.

STILL JAZZED FROM our engagement, Ali and I set a tentative date for our wedding. May 1995. A little less than a year away. We asked Ellen, a professional photographer, to take our photo. And, on a particularly warm, breezy day, we climbed up on the roof with a few beers and a kitchen chair. Ali had on a light, sleeveless top and a skirt, and I wore a white T-shirt and chinos. We were both barefoot. I remember feeling awkward and uncomfortable at the beginning of the shoot. The beer helped, and so did Ellen's easy professionalism behind a camera; pretty soon we were falling naturally into poses. My favorite shot catches Ali and me in a moment of true intimacy. She is sitting on a pair of throw pillows, one knee up, a hand lightly grasping her ankle. I am crouching behind her, hands on knees. Ali's other hand is up to my face. She has turned her face to mine, and I am leaning into the cup of her hand. Our eyes are closed. Ali is smiling serenely; I look calm, almost as if ready to fall asleep. Behind us, out of focus, Ann Arbor's downtown buildings mix into a hazy screen of trees. The sky a white drop cloth tacked to a wall.

I like the photo for its on-high vantage point: it places us in the clouds. But I also see two people turning to each other for support. I see Ali's love for me, and how I have let myself relax into it.

Soon after the photo shoot, however, we had a call from my mother with bad news. Her mother was about to die of the cancer she had been battling for years. Could I come back east to see her one last time? I made sure it was okay to bring Ali, for we wanted to carry with us the news of our engagement. It seemed important to include others in our happiness.

We stayed at my grandmother's for a few days, our visit filled with small talk and errands run as if they were sacred rites (which, in a way, they were). We did what we could to make her time bearable, but she was the one doing the looking after, the one being thoughtful.

My grandmother's faith in her Catholic God surrounded her in an aura. Having been raised without religion, I had never been able to trust this aspect of my grandmother. (When people asked me my religion I'd always tell them the Woody Allen joke about his parents: one was an agnostic and the other an atheist, and they couldn't decide which religion *not* to bring him up in.) I had only been able to see the social side of my grandparents' churchgoing; the dinner prayers seemed rushed and insincere. But during those last few days I witnessed her faith. She seemed ready to die, unafraid, secure with her place in things.

After our return to Ann Arbor, we called my grandmother's frequently to check in. Along with her sisters and brothers, my mother was taking turns watching over her. The last few hours it had been only Mom and her younger sister Maureen. We got the call as we were preparing dinner. When I heard my mother's voice, I knew Grandma had died. There was something strange about my mother's voice: it was hers and it wasn't. She sounded as if she was just a girl.

I was hit with the insight that the mother I knew had died, too, and that she had been reborn as my sister, whose voice was speaking to me over a thousand miles, both utterly foreign and shockingly familiar.

"It's okay," I said. "She was ready."

"I know," she said back. And then she started crying.

"She sounded like a girl," I said later to Ali. "Like she was seventeen."

When my father's father had died, I had been unable to process the significance of the event. I had loved the man, but his death did not penetrate deeply into my consciousness. I could not come close to imagining what my father had felt losing his own father. But now that my grandmother was dead, and Pat, my father's wife, might also die, I began to feel the full weight of mortality. This seemed even more reason to be with Ali.

BY THE END of the summer we had moved across town into the house near Burns Park that Marc and Ellen owned. They were moving to Georgia and said we could rent their house as long as we needed. We had decided that our wedding would be traditionally Jewish with a New Age spin. We'd have a rabbi—a longtime friend of Ali's family and her Jewish chaplain in high school—but we'd also incorporate other rituals. We spent many evenings planning the ceremony. All the while, Ali creating a hand-quilted chuppah under which we would be married.

Each week brought new decisions. What caterer. What kind of cake. Where in the Climo backyard to set up the receiving line. Ali decided to wear her mother's wedding dress; everyone went along, at first reluctantly, when I announced I wasn't wearing a tie with my suit. Mom and Charter were planning a party at the Scruton Pond community house as an alternative to the standard rehearsal dinner. Dad said that Pat seemed to be responding well to chemotherapy. Her cancer was in remission and, if all went well, she would be able to make it to the ceremony.

—————

THE NIGHT BEFORE our wedding, my parents are hanging out at the community house party, smoking cigarettes and trading easy banter. The miraculous sight of Mom and Dad in the same room creates a temporary (if illusory) feeling that my life has been healed and has come full circle. When Charter and my father stop to talk at the buffet table, I take Ali aside.

"Look," I tell her. "That's my life coming together."

"You don't need your parents to get back together, Bash, for your life to be whole."

"I know. It's just wild seeing them in the same place."

Neither of us has seen Pat yet. When I have a moment free, I ask my father. He says that she's still doing well but won't be coming to the wedding. I don't get it.

"The relationship is over," he tells me. *The patient in remission but the marriage terminal.*

I go and find my brother at the pond to tell him.

"Can you believe it?"

Bill doesn't answer. He's looking out at the still water, at the circle of trees that enclose it. I am not sure if he's heard me. Back up at the community house, the band is warming up.

When Charter returned to his Zen meditation practice, one end of the community house was converted into a *zendo*, complete with tatami mats, sitting cushions, and an altar. Now, three times a week, Charter lights a fire in the stove before going to bed, then wakes up at seven for the morning sit, stoking up the coals that smolder overnight. I woke up early enough this morning to join him for a sit, bringing a cup of coffee to stay awake. We walked down the dirt road together, not talking. I stretched in a corner of the community house while he stoked the fire. Then we settled on our mats, Charter hit the bell softly, and I closed my eyes and tried to quiet my mind.

My father is standing off on his own, smoking a cigarette. What do I expect from him, anyway? It is always the same with him when it comes to women. I love the man, but he drives me crazy. What I don't know: in a year his health will deteriorate to the extent where surgery is necessary to clean out the arteries in his legs; the procedure going so poorly that he spends eight hours on the table, emerging from the anesthesia a nonsmoker. In two years, after what to everyone feels like a miraculous recovery—in which he has been scared into a new, healthy lifestyle—my father will die suddenly from either a massive heart attack or a brain aneurysm, dead too young just like his own father. Whatever it is coming down like a fist to knock the man clear out of his life.

IT RAINS EARLY the morning of our wedding, but the bad weather passes by the time the caterers arrive. The tents are up, the food under wraps. The guests arrive in bunches and mass down by the altar set up in the grape arbor. Ali and I join our wedding party out behind the garage. The cellist is laying out the first few notes of the Bach solo he's been paid to play. Everyone is looking up the hill for a glimpse of the bride. The time has finally come.

But Ali is held up at the garage, hidden behind the bush, waiting for our chuppah-bearers to gain control over the large, unwieldy quilt and its quartet of walking-stick-sized poles. Alan and Lisel, Bryan and Jodi, each of our oldest and newest friends, are struggling to keep the canopy afloat in the recently picked-up wind, while the rest of us discuss the best way to proceed. Ali keeps peeking through the bushes, trying to make out faces in the group below. I am beginning to question my suit choice. But then someone comes up with the bright idea of holding the bottom ends of the poles inward. Problem solved. The music swells to its climax and, after a moment of silence, starts again. Finally, we are moving.

Ali and I walk behind the chuppah at the back of the small scrum that is our wedding party. Ali's parents, Larry and Diane, come first, then Marie and Charter, then my father, conspicuously alone, looking dapper in his gray suit. Our brothers and sisters follow, all smiles and firework nerves, trailed by a few more close friends. In front of us, the rest of our family and friends rise up in ragged unison. Shielding their eyes en masse against the latest surge of sunlight, they wait expectantly for us to make our way to the grape arbor, to join the rabbi in its shade. As through a magical gate, the parents walk under the chuppah and take their seats, all three men stooping a little to make it under its temporary threshold. Then the chuppah-bearers bring the chuppah to the arbor and station themselves halfway under it, the wide side of the quilt facing the guests. When the siblings arrive, there is a handoff of the poles, and the oldest and newest friends take their seats.

As I wait under the arbor for my bride to complete the last leg of her journey, looking out at the crowd and reminding myself to take mental photographs, my father's penetrating gaze comes into focus in among the field of faces. His expression softens around the mouth as I watch him, a small smile forming in his eyes. He is thinking up something, I can tell. (Later, my father will turn to my mother in the receiving line and say: "I notice there was no mention of the deity formally known as Yahweh.")

Then the bride is passing across the lawn in slow motion, the trees behind her rustling in the breeze. The attention of a hundred and fifty people drapes on her like sunlight. And, indeed, she is beautiful in her mom's wedding dress. She looks happy and a little scared. When she arrives at my side, Ali gives me a nervous look, then grasps my hand. Together we step under the chuppah to join Rabbi Gendler, who is standing ready, a look of serenity on his face backed by the subtlest of Cheshire Cat smiles.

To my right, Ali's sisters, Amy and Elana, are both gazing intently at their oldest sister, searching her face for clues. They seem curious about what it is like to get married. To my left, brother Bill smiles back at me, as when we rode amusement park rides as kids and he held my hand and put on his brave face to help me through. Manny—my adopted brother, my kid brother—is staring off into the forest, happy to be holding one of the poles, and, as always, looking good doing it. And now the rabbi is giving his words of greeting. I can barely hear them. So much crammed into the moment that it is hard to focus. Our carefully worded vows have vanished from my mind; my suit jacket feels as heavy as one of those X-ray vests they drape over you at the doctor's.

Everywhere I see old friends and new, aunts and uncles, cousins. My grandmother, Mary, sitting beside my father, beaming. Behind her, Ali's grandparents, Sam and Esther. Across the aisle: my aunt Charlotte and her husband, John, decked out in sunglasses. Everywhere I look the two sides of my family are joined together for a day, mixing effortlessly into Ali's. Something I never thought I'd see—my cloven family brought together in ceremonial time.

And when I look back at the rabbi, he is smiling. He has been waiting for me to return. *Here I am.*

THE TRADITIONAL JEWISH wedding has at its center seven sacred blessings. We had asked Dad to reinterpret the seventh as part of the wedding ceremony. He wrote about it in a published journal entry:

> Sebastian has asked me to give—to reinvent—one of the traditional blessings for his wedding to Ali.
>
> I who've blessed my marriages with divorce as a man shoots a broken-legged horse.

The traditional translation listed the seventh blessing as *ten shades of joy*. My father found the phrase thrilling but concluded that the actual list (bridegroom and bride, love and fellowship, etc.) was dull, "striding up the ramp in pairs not to the Ark but to the Love Boat." He decided, after some deliberation about the challenges of form, to write a poem in ten stanzas, "of ten lines each. Pentameter, natch. Perhaps each stanza might conclude with a couplet as an instance of knot-tying. 'Ten Shades of Joy.' "

My father did not read a poem to us at our wedding, though. He stood up, instead, and spoke elegantly about the small blessings of marriage. At the end of his brief oration, he urged us to expand this idea of "ten shades of joy" into what the Buddhists call the "ten thousand things." He was eloquent, as usual. But more importantly, by speaking off the cuff, he was being authentic.

He did write a version of that poem, however, with only a few lines of the original version remaining. It shows up in his last book, *After All*. In the poem, he's sitting alone at a bar the night of my wedding. He's trying not to feel sorry for himself, happy that his sons have both found partners.

May 28th, 1995

The bride, groom (my son) and their friends gathered
somewhere else to siphon the wedding's last
drops from their tired elders. Over a glass
of chardonnay I ignored my tattered,
companionable glooms (this took some will:
I've ended three marriages by divorce
as a man shoots his broken-legged horse)
and wished my two sons and their families
something I couldn't have, or keep, myself.
The rueful pluck we take with us to bars
or church, the morbid fellowship of woe—
I've had my fill of it. I wouldn't mope
through my son's happiness or further fear
my own. Well, what instead? Well, something else.

On our wedding night, Ali and I came down from the Andover Inn's bridal suite, too amped to retire right away. My father was at the bar, and a handful of other relatives were hanging out in the bar's lounge. Ali, glowing, still in her dress, floated over to the lounge to "siphon the last drops." I sat down at the bar with my dad and ordered shots of whiskey. I wanted to know what had happened between him and Pat.

"I thought you guys had gotten through the hard part," I said.

"Guess not."

"Did she leave you? Why?"

These were not answerable questions. Dad had only good things to say about Pat, of course, how brave she had been through the year of chemotherapy, the five weeks of radiation. And I was proud of my father for being there during that time, but I didn't blame Pat for calling it off once she'd made it through safely. The trip must have been exhausting.

That night at the bar, it didn't dawn on me that my father was probably painfully aware of his own mortality. When his own father had died suddenly of a heart attack, he had been in his mid-sixties, healthy and hale. By his own admission, my father had had a harder and slower time than he expected recapturing his balance after his father's death. (He wrote in a letter to a friend, "In my experience, one's parents die over and over." In the same letter he describes watching *Boris Godunov* on archival tape. Boris Christoff was singing the death scene, "which requires the bass to keel over at the end of a kind of mad scene. My eyes filled with tears. It was beautifully sung, for that matter, but it was my father's heart attack I was watching.")

I wish I had seen that fear in my father. Maybe then I would have told him that I wished his father had been alive for our wedding. That I would have liked my grandfather and Ali to meet. Dad would have said: "Me, too, kiddo. Me, too."

But I didn't.

~

August 25, 1995, Ann Arbor
I was out walking the afternoon of my thirtieth birthday. It had been a good year, one in which I had gotten married, worked hard

on my writing, and had gone to therapy consistently and seriously. Ali and I were happy in our lives. My teaching was going well and Ali was plugging away at her dissertation. Later that evening Ali and I would go out for a fancy dinner, but first I wanted a few hours on my own.

My plan was to revisit the tract of injured land behind the graveyard that I'd begun calling "my property." It had been a while since I last made the trek. We lived on the other side of town now, and I had to cross through the university to get there. But I didn't mind. It felt nostalgic to pass over the tracks on First, to cut through the backs of the lumberyard, the Montessori school, and the car parts factory (the last of its kind in the area).

When I made it to the foot of the hill where Fountain meets Miller, a familiar excitement rose in my body. I nodded at a man tending his lawn, steering clear of the little girl wobbling downhill on her training-wheeled bike. I strode down the center of the street, hands at sides, fingers extended, eyes straight ahead but scanning the periphery. My awareness placed in the balls of my feet, I dropped my tall man's balance down a notch into the pelvis. I was fielding with all my senses, with sight and second sight, smell, taste, hearing. The breeze picked up and turned the leaves over, exposing their undersides, and the air filled with a muted "swish" sound. Everything was in movement—a squirrel circling the base of a tree, a chickadee out of a bush, a young man coiling a hose—all part of a synchronous sound track. I was strolling under a promenade of trees, dappled light filtering through the leaves and dropping on my shoulders like grace.

Just as I arrived at the cemetery gate, the sun slipped out from behind clouds and turned a bright light on the day. Enraptured, I stepped into the graveyard, paid my respects to the woman I always imagined to be sitting in the gatehouse window, then headed directly for the young man's gravestone that marked the entrance.

There had been some rain the last few days, so the stone was covered with damp dirt. I knelt down and cleared off the gravestone, rubbing my fingers over the engraved letters. But when I passed over the lip of the hill this time and started down into the outback, there was a fence with a "No Trespassing" sign hanging askew in its wire mesh. I dropped to my knees and tested the bottom of the fence, partially torn free at one post, then started to pull at the flap. But something inside me balked. I wanted to go in, of course, to move forward past the obstacle as though it were just another inconvenience. But another voice, the second thought behind the quick-deciding first, told me to go around, to find someplace else.

It was a clear voice, one I hadn't heard before, and so I listened, backing up and making my way out of the graveyard, walking down through an unfamiliar neighborhood of two- and three-story homes. Maybe I'd stumble upon that bird sanctuary a friend told me about. Right off Highway 14, he said, with beautiful hills, a patch of old growth, and long walking paths.

Since I was heading in that direction already, I continue making my way through the network of back roads; and soon I find myself crossing under the highway and walking up to the entrance of the sanctuary, proud to have found the place, glad to be walking into new territory. And indeed I spend a few blissful hours up in the forest: stepping over small streams, looking for birds. I even come across a shelter someone has built out of gathered branches.

Crouching there for a while, I watch, as a fox might, two runners making their loud, chatty way through the trees.

Later, in the restaurant, over a birthday glass of wine, I related to Ali the story of the fence and my decision to move around it.

"About the second thought business," I told her. "I have always gone with my first inclination. Probably out of conditioning. I've never been the kind of person who used tools well, or sang beautifully, or who knew all the names of the trees. I always thought I should know what I wanted without having to think twice."

Ali wanted to say something, but I put out my hand for her not to speak.

"It is like with sharks," I said, "and how they need to be constantly in motion."

I poured some more wine.

"Now I go back to the same place and all of a sudden—"

"Everything is 'all of a sudden' with you, Matthews," Ali said.

And I knew she was right, and that I should have laughed. "Yeah, I know, I know. But all of a sudden there's this fence and I have to decide, but not a quick decision, instead a thought-out one."

That was it. Ali couldn't wait anymore. She had to break in.

"You were able to slow down and see how you really *felt*. You weren't simply reacting."

I nodded. I sat back and watched my new wife spin out meaning. It was her forte.

"The fence told you that what was there before, that what you discovered and returned for, wasn't necessarily there anymore, or important in the same way."

The waitress arrived with our meal. She turned each hot plate a little for the proper presentation. Ali had ordered glazed pork chops and garlic mashed potatoes. I was having a rustic risotto. It all looked and smelled delicious. For the time being, there was nothing more to say. We toasted, instead, silently, on my turning thirty, on being together, and on a new outlook. Then we started eating.

Goodbye Porkpie Hat

You must release as much of this hoard
as you can, little by little, in perfect time,
as the work of the body becomes a body of work.

WILLIAM MATTHEWS, "Mingus in Diaspora"

I t's easy to see why the jazz saxophonist Lester Young was one of my father's heroes. "The Pres," as he was affectionately dubbed by Billie Holiday, was an intensely private man, a lover of a well-turned phrase, a natty dresser. His style of play was characterized by its light, swinging sound and by the way it drifted over the ground beat of the rhythm section. As my father put it in one of his essays, Young "played with an unmatched tenderness, as if suffering and pleasure were impossible without each other." All this could be said about William Matthews and his poetry.

It goes further. Both men died young after struggling with substance abuse; both were melancholic, loved by women, witty, pacifists at heart. These are, of course, surface similarities: Young was a black man, a musician, a heroin addict; my father white, a poet, a drinker and smoker. Their eras, their milieus, were radically different. My father was never in the service, for instance, or dishonorably discharged, or ever the target of an overt, pervasive racism as was Young; and the Pres, to the best of my knowledge, never went to a prep school in Massachusetts, nor did he translate Horace, or shoot a hundred foul shots every afternoon for a summer.

Nevertheless, since we are chosen as much by our early heroes as we choose them, it is easy to imagine my father as a teenager picking up the saxophone for the first time and right away tilting the horn sideways in Pres' signature, off-kilter manner.

THERE'S A POEM my father wrote about Young. He was in his early thirties when he wrote it, but it could easily be read as prophetic of his own life, and death. The opening lines read:

> It's 1958. Lester Young minces
> out, spraddle-legged as if pain
> were something he could step over
> by raising his groin, and begins
> to play. Soon he'll be dead.

I've seen my father walk out to give a reading like that. Long-time friends gasping at the sight of his bloated face, or quietly taking in his new limp, would search me out later at the reception to ask about his health. They'd ask, "Is he smoking too much?" They'd say, "He looks so old," worry composing their faces. But I knew they were also seeing their own mortality in his crumbling health, and so I kept my speculations to myself.

The poem goes on to describe Young's deteriorating playing as "all tone now and tone / slurring toward the center of each note." The more ruinous Young became, the more ruinous his playing.

Which isn't always true for the poet. (For maybe one of the more salient distinctions to make between two such men concerns their relation to their instrument and to the breath it requires to both maintain and free it.) You see, my father's tone never diminished or blurred, never caved in on itself or grew thick in the fingers. It only got honed. Cruelly, he died at the height of his powers.

There's an argument that the later Young recordings, though technically flawed—skill and verve gummed up by heroin—were more powerful by their being more lived in. Something about the downfall of a man turned alchemically into the blues. The same thing was said about the downward arc of Billie Holiday's voice. My father would have fought the temptation to side with this sentiment. He would have said something intelligent about why such an idea was half right, and then he'd put on an old Teddy Wilson recording with Lady Day and the Pres sitting in—some number like "I Can't Get Started" or "Miss Brown to You," one of those shiny blue locomotives of sound—and sit there tapping his foot, eyes half closed, letting the joyous music prove just how wrong you were.

The reason my father could write so well about jazz was because he had led the working poet's life so fully—the reading tours, the visiting poet gigs, the conferences—and this kind of artist-for-hire approach afforded him knowledge about some of the essential aspects of jazz life: the glamour (the tedium) of travel, the companionship of comrades, nights in hotels and long rides to shabby rooms, late hours, fans who loved you or wanted a piece of you mostly for all the wrong reasons. The rest he learned from books.

And let's not pass over his ability to listen closely to a record.

Or his going to countless live performances, sitting in on the sets both as eager young man and knowing middle-aged gentleman with the graying mustache and the money for a good bottle of wine (say, the '89 pinot noir right here at the bottom of the list); or his knowing something about that strange, bitter stalemate that gets called race relations in this country, and his having the courage to say something about it.

Where did he get the nerve to do that? Maybe it's from the hours he spent playing league ball, the only white guy on the team; or growing up in Cincinnati, one of those strange half-southern, half-midwestern cities where the racial divide is as narrow as a single street and, at the same time, as wide as the Mississippi. Of course, that's not enough to warrant any white man putting on blackface. So maybe, most importantly, it's his poet's imagination—a little empathy, an intuitive sympathy bordering on thievery—tuned so often, and so earnestly, to the black man's experience that, though it may not speak directly for anything but his own sense of things—or any white man's alienation from his black brethren—nevertheless had an authentic ring to it. He wasn't pretending to be black—no more than Gerry Mulligan was when he stepped up to his solo beside Coleman Hawkins—just allowing some of the history and truth and energy of that great musical legacy to flow through him.

My father wrote well about jazz because he had taken what he had learned from its masters—Louis, Duke, Bird, Pres, Coltrane, Mingus, Miles—much of what he knew as cool. And he had a good enough ear to approximate its rhythms in his own verse. And, damn it, because he had soul.

In one of his several Mingus poems, my father writes about seeing the great bassist and bandleader at the Showplace. It's 1960 and he's only eighteen, coming into New York City on weekends to watch the master rule over his Jazz Workshop. In an interview for the first issue of *Brilliant Corners*, he describes those performances as "not nightclub 'entertainment,' but more like a master class at Juilliard." In the poem "Mingus at the Showplace," Mingus stops the band in mid-number to fire the pianist. He turns to the audience and informs them: "We have suffered a diminuendo in personnel." Later, after the first set maybe, the young, big-eared poet is up at the bar and hands the great musician and composer one of his own poems. After reading it, Mingus says, "There's a lot of that going around."

I never could tell if this encounter actually took place, or if it was only half true. (Say they sat beside each other at the bar once, the way Kerouac brags of grabbing a beer over the head of Charlie Parker in a San Francisco juke joint.) But the myth of it feels right. My father says in that interview, "I knew in some visceral way I was witnessing a genius at work." Did I know those late nights that I was witnessing a genius at work? I am not sure. But I do know, for sure, and with that artificial clarity that hindsight affords, that I, too, was that big-eared kid—like father, like son—summoning up his nerve to publish his own paltry attempts at art making to an audience of one.

For all these reasons, and for a few, private, complicated ones of my own, I knew what music had to be played at my father's funeral. Charlie Mingus' haunting elegy for Pres would be mine to my father. "Goodbye Porkpie Hat" had to be his send-off.

.   .   .

MY FATHER WRITES that in the blues, and in life, pain and joy eat off each other's plates. This is why I chose a second funeral song, Horace Silver's "Song for My Father," to counterbalance Mingus' wrenching elegy for Lester Young. By playing a joyous song following a sad one, I hoped to lift the gathering, if only for a minute, out of its collective grief. But what I hear now when I play these songs back to back is how each holds some of the other's essence in its heart.

On the version of "Goodbye Porkpie Hat" off *Ah Um*, Mingus highlights two saxophonists, Booker Ervin and John Handy, and throughout the song their complementary tones harmonize the somber melody. It opens and closes with earthbound trudging—as if the musicians were following a casket down a street. There's reverence in the song, for sure, but there's yearning, too. The song's cup is mostly filled with blue notes and solemnity.

In the middle of the song, however, Handy's saxophone breaks free from this procession and lifts up and away to soar awhile in the clouds. It's as if he has become the reincarnated spirit of Young, let loose after a hard life and a bitter battle with drugs. Eventually he comes back down, rejoining the band to moan out the song's final, descending dirgelike cry. Handy's voice is immediately subsumed in the band's song, which in turn has become infused by his birdlike soaring. What starts off as sad, blue yearning winds up threaded through with joy and hope.

On the contrary, "Song for My Father" is infectiousness embodied. Right from the start, the song breaks into the giddy running-skip of a young boy let out of school early. The trumpet and saxophone are out front here (Carmell Jones and Joe Henderson, respectively), plaintive and jaunty, propelled by the bossa-nova-inflected cadences of Silver's piano. Their two voices meld into one joyous call. Soon Silver takes the solo lead, moving ahead in light, playful runs that glide over a bluesy, soulful bounce. When Henderson takes the baton back from Silver, he breaks into a trot, swinging loose and free. After the solo, the band comes back around to the song's melody and rides it out for a few choruses while Silver dances around the walked dog of the bass line. Then, gradually winding down, the song comes to the softest hard stop imaginable. A book closing.

Listening to this song is like thinking back on happy childhood days. (Silver himself makes this connection in the album's liner notes.) Like sitting on a sunny porch with time to kill and a cool drink at hand. The subject here is happiness but the vehicle is memory and so the tone gets shot through with wistfulness, with some of the "ruinous nostalgia" the poet Weldon Kees talks about. The exuberance of youth reflected upon from the vantage point of middle age. A blue bossa nova.

When the recording of "Goodbye Porkpie Hat" ended, the roomful of mourners—friends and family, students and colleagues—sat in silence. Then "Song for My Father" came on and, I tell you, for a moment there we were all walked out the door and shown the wide green world, the sun out and the day open. I was sadder than I had ever been before, but at the same time—and this is the part my father would have understood the most—I was also happy, alive with little pinpricks of excitement and expectation.

THOSE FIRST FEW weeks after the funeral, our friends in Ann Arbor stopped by to make sure we were doing okay. They asked after our health, brought us food, invited us to Thanksgiving dinner. The weeks clicked past, and we did whatever it took to get through—letting bills go unpaid, dishes unwashed. Slept a lot.

As I went about my numb routine, I couldn't help revisiting that string of surreal days after my father's death. I kept flashing back on the long afternoon we spent at the funeral home—making arrangements, deciding on the coffin, picking flowers, choosing the room for the service. How the *Times* obit guy tracked us down for more biographical data. The way the innocuous "grieving rooms" were tactfully situated, mazelike, around the funeral home's lobby, making the place feel like a somber brothel or a swanky massage parlor. The inconspicuous men standing around looking like neutered FBI flunkies. Then there was the comment the courteous mortician made as we first shook hands: "I am so sorry to have to meet you." A phrase my father would have relished and, later (as now), skewered to the page.

I remembered, too, the strange moment near the end of the funeral service: how, at Celia's request, we played a recording of the *scena penultima* in Mozart's *Don Giovanni*. Russell Banks had tried to dissuade her from this choice, concerned that Don Giovanni's descent into hell might be inappropriate for the occasion. But Celia said it had been the last music she and Bill had listened to together. So we went ahead. I watched the crowd as Giovanni's strong baritone rose in defiance against the Stone Guest, refusing, as he was dying, to repent for a life of infidelities and excess. A few heads lifted in disbelief; a look of amusement passed over one mourner's carefully composed face. *Could this be?* Yes, indeed. A perversely perfect irony befitting my father's sense of humor, his life and loves.

And that first evening in the city, how lost Ali and I felt at not being able to stay in my dad's apartment. How broken up and inconsolable Celia was. How devastated Susan and Mary were, both trying to hunker down into the grief and stay balanced. We were all doing our best to get things worked out, taking turns playing the front man. When my mother made it in after a day of hard travel, Ali finally broke down. She told me later that she felt as though an adult had finally showed up. That she could be the kid.

My brother flew in the next day with his wife, Rochelle. Charter arrived later that night. Everyone met at Susan's apartment in the Village, then went out for drinks at the White Horse Tavern, joined by Dad's old friends Russ and Chase. We were an odd assortment, a gathering my dad would never have chosen, but a family nonetheless.

Only once during those hectic days in New York did Ali and I manage to be alone. We went out for dinner, deciding on the Chinese place near Lincoln Center that Dad had introduced us to the year before. He had urged us to try their lemon chicken, assuring us of a pleasurable experience. He wasn't wrong (he was rarely, if ever, wrong about matters of cuisine). We ordered the dish again that night and, even though the management had changed in the meantime, it was just as good. We ate in embarrassing haste, discovering with each bite just how famished we were. The waiters averted their eyes as they passed.

. . .

AND THEN ALI and I still had to face the sobering task of winding up my dad's affairs. The semester had come to a close; when else would we have such a long string of days to get the work done? So we flew into Newark and caught a shuttle into the city, this time with a key to the place and no police escort. My father's lonely apartment, covered in a fine layer of dust, and the difficult task of cleanup awaited us.

We decided to begin with his daily life. I returned a month's accumulation of phone calls while Ali attacked the mail, which had grown into a mammoth pile overflowing the coffee table onto the floor. It quickly became apparent that the daily "goings-on" of my father's life were still moving forward. There were unanswered calls, broken appointments, letters and bills. Dinner reservations left dangling. Opera tickets in his wallet. And the phone continued to ring. Old friends, students I'd never heard of, from twenty years back, were in town and wanted to come over for the famous talk and the equally famous bottle of wine. At each call, I had to keep telling people the news. *No, my father is not here,* I'd have to say. *This is his son. I am sorry to have to tell you. . . .* All of a sudden, I was the cop in the strange man's apartment, answering the phone to disbelief and rage and shock, doing my best to console. Trying my best at this odd job of managing a death.

Just when Ali and I were about to lose it, my brother flew in for a few days. It was time to divvy up my dad's things. Susan joined us for an afternoon, coming up from the West Village to sort through her brother's books, looking for keepsakes for herself and her mother. She let us decide on the big stuff. Luckily, Bill and I were in agreement; we wanted to make sure things went smoothly. The oriental rugs, surprisingly, were the hardest decisions. The artwork painted by old friends.

Maybe it was too early to be making those decisions. Celia couldn't bring herself to come to the apartment, never mind choose objects she wanted to keep. Her shock and loss were too great to allow her any sober decisions. For my part, I wanted to come back someday—in a year or two maybe—and deal with it all then. But we had begun the process; we did the best we could under the circumstances.

Much of our energy was spent resolving the private matters of a man who felt he had bought himself another ten years by giving up smoking. The unsigned will, the recently completed manuscript of poems, a deal to buy a house, a box of unread student manuscripts.

One of the ways we discovered to pay tribute and do some housecleaning at the same time was to give away my father's possessions to friends and organizations. Poets House in Manhattan received most of his poetry books. His old prep school received the lion's share of his fiction and biography collection. Sean, one of his favorite students from City College, inherited his entire jazz collection on cassette. I made sure Russ received Dad's vast tie collection, for he had mentioned at the memorial how the ties served to illustrate the man—elegant, colorful, abundant, a little worn at the edges.

By New Year's, most of Dad's furniture had been crated off; only books and records were left, arbitrary piles of clothes and cookware. We slept on a futon in the corner. Mornings we'd wake up and continue taking down his carefully constructed world of things postcard by postcard, CD by CD, dismantling a life silently like workmen set to a task. The hardest thing about this whole closing-up-shop process was how it got in the way of moving through the grief. I was getting things done, doing the right thing, when what I really wanted was some time away, a little room to take in this drastic newness.

THERE WERE TWO memorial readings in New York City: one by my father's former students, the other by friends and colleagues. More than a dozen tribute poems appeared in literary journals and anthologies, along with reminiscences and a growing number of critical pieces that attempted to sum up my father's body of work.

At the tribute held at the New School in Manhattan, many of my father's friends and colleagues showed up to read from his work, to say something about him, or to recount a story. Gerald Stern called him "our soul." Richard Tillinghast remembered him sartorially. "You can always tell a gentleman by his shoes," his mother once told him. "Bill's shoes were elegant and expensive and also very comfortable."

His oldest friends remembered him through his loves. Russell Banks talked of his love of jazz and basketball. Daniel Halpern spoke of his love of cooking. And his old friend Stanley Plumly started his reading by saying, "He saved my life many times." When it was my turn, I stood up and read a list of the "favorite things" my dad passed down to my brother and me—from the Marx Brothers to Bob Marley, Travis McGee to Muhammad Ali, Coltrane to Dylan, Easy Rawlins to *Rigoletto*.

The night ended with a tape of my father reading a few of his poems. The first poem was one of my favorites, "Mood Indigo." Hearing his voice broadcast throughout the auditorium was eerie, made even more so by the poor quality of the recording. It was sped up, making his voice sound higher and more nasal than it actually was. I wanted to stand up and say, "That's not my father's voice."

There's a poem in *Time & Money* entitled "Bob Marley's Hair." It's set on a plane heading for Kingston, and Marley's cancer-riddled body lies in a coffin in the plane's cargo hold:

> *In the cabin on the same flight*
> *Marley's mother kept the dreadlocks*
> *like a folded flag, or dog tags,*
> *on her lap in a box.*

For me, my father's voice symbolizes his life. Like Marley's dreads, the voice embodied the spirit of the man. Now, as a way to remember him, to recapture a little of his essence, I play one of the tapes I have of him reading. His deep, sonorous voice with the slight lisp at the frayed edges of syllables ambles into the room; and, for a moment, I am back in the presence of my father.

TO MANY OF his students and colleagues, I imagine, my father was considered an easy touch. He wanted to please too much, was so compelled to be a good citizen of the arts, that he couldn't turn down the endless requests for recommendations, blurbs, and manuscript readings. A softy maybe, but not a pushover. Here's a telling story. A friend of his who owned a goat asked if my father would like to milk her. My dad was game to try but the goat only went into its stall three-quarters of the way. The friend, sensing my father's frustration, said, "You can push her, it's part of her manners." Later, back in the city, Dad observed, "New York manners are a lot like that goat's." He said it with admiration in his voice. A midwesterner by birth, my father liked the push.

My father was a quietly formal man; his need for privacy bordered on secrecy. It wasn't just about good manners, or simply a matter of breeding—that he came from an upper-middle-class, midwestern family or attended boarding school—no, he was one of those shy children who behind closed doors had mastered inadequacy by willfully ordering his life. He moved elegantly through a shifting landscape of indiscretions.

The affairs, of course. But he kept his money matters close to his chest, too. Bill and I were told conflicting stories about family money, inheritance. As part of a pact, my father burned the letters received from his mother and asked her to do the same for him. Like a spy, my father compartmentalized his life, keeping large parts of himself separate from the others. You could say he chose a life that allowed him to be in more than one place at a time. He put on masks, played roles. But do we really choose our lifestyle, or does it instead form itself to us, taking shape in our habits, our words, our private thoughts? And how much do we inherit?

As a poet, my father was a self-confessed hoarder of words; such privacies went with the territory. But I was more than a little surprised to discover that at least half of the letters in his literary estate—more than two decades' worth—were missing. Either he deliberately threw them away—which he swore to a close friend that he did—or lost track of them during that desperate string of moves in the eighties. He also threw away drafts of his poems, not interested in the idea of some future scholar retracing his poetic steps to discover a pearl of insight. He wanted you to read the finished poems. ("Literary criticism is easy to judge, after all," he writes in an essay. "It either leads you usefully into a given text or not.")

It's not surprising that my father's poetry is crowded with awkward humanity—with loners, young lovers, animals, street people, children, young men darting across Broadway at night. "Fellow oddballs," as he toasts in a poem by that name: "Here's to us, / morose at dances and giggly in committee . . ." In one of his poems my father calls his own father "a mild, democratic man." The same could be said about him. And not because he was any great populist—he wasn't—but because he insisted on numbering himself one of the crowd.

My father never felt comfortable talking about himself. At parties, he'd turn the tables on the questioner or dive into a discourse on one of his many pet subjects—the Knicks, opera, jazz, cooking, wine, Horace, truffle pigs. He didn't mind the attention; he simply didn't like divulging too much of his private life. (Though often an autobiographical poet, he was never merely confessional.)

Then again, he liked to show off. He probably wouldn't have seen it that way, but he did. I think he got caught up in the pageantry of his loves. For instance, at dinners he would make sure his guests heard the whole story of each course, inviting them in to witness the little flourishes required to complete each stage of preparation. He didn't expect you to applaud, but it wouldn't have been out of place either. We were all part of the studio audience for the Bill Matthews cooking show.

I remember one time Ali and I were helping with dessert for that night's dinner. Ali's job was to pit the cherries. My father proudly fished out his special cherry pitter, handing it to Ali with a flourish, casually informing us that the instrument made "an excellent stocking stuffer." Later, leafing through one of his many cookbooks, I came upon something that made me laugh out loud. I pulled Ali aside and pointed out the passage. "This unique cherry pitter," the official banter read, "makes an excellent stocking stuffer."

⟶

ONCE WE DECIDED to sell it, my dad's apartment went quickly. The deal was completed within a month, the papers signed in March of 1998. Our lawyer even arranged it so I didn't have to be present at the signing. At first I appreciated this gesture, but as the day for turning over the property came near I became more and more agitated. I didn't want to give up the apartment, I realized, without going back one last time. It was hard not to see our emptying my father's apartment only a month after his death as a kind of theft. And though I kept telling myself that this evacuation had been somehow necessary, it still felt as though we had defiled my father's inner sanctum.

So, the April following his death, I was walking up Broadway again. It was one of those perfect spring days in the city, the sun out in full force and a light breeze passing up from Riverside Park. People were lit up in the sunlight, their dresses and coat jackets lifted lightly in the wind. I felt like a walk-on in one of Woody Allen's Manhattan valentines.

Luckily, the key was waiting for me at the desk. (The new owners of the apartment generously allowing me the whole afternoon alone.) The young guy behind the counter recognized me and arranged his face to approximate a sympathetic understanding of grief. I smiled at the guy. A jazz bassist studying the philosophy of science, he was always one of my father's favorites.

Since the elevator had been replaced and there was no longer a need for a doorman to operate it, I decided to take the stairs. I enjoyed passing up through the shafts of light; there were paintings in the stairwell, abstract watercolors and oil portraits painted years ago by one of the doormen. The old National Rifle Association sticker was still stuck to my father's door. It had been his idea of theft deterrence, I guess—the poet's alarm system. But the lock was new, and the old welcome mat gone. There was even a blank space where the *Attention: Chat Lunatique* sign used to be.

After I inserted the key into the new lock and stepped inside, I was surprised to find boxes in the hall and an odd pile of books in my dad's study. *Hadn't we cleared everything out?* I spent the next couple of hours trying to connect with my father's spirit, trying to find a way to say goodbye. But there was nothing tangible to hold on to. It was as though he had "stepped into the quicksilver of a mirror," as Lawrence Durrell describes a character's sudden death in *Justine*. I simply sat in a corner and let myself feel exhaustion settle over my body. I wanted to cry but felt too self-conscious. So I sat there, eyes closed, until I remembered an afternoon from that last trip to Seattle with Dad.

We had all gone out to Vashon Island, driving our cars onto one of the famous ferries, sitting up on the observation deck for bad coffee and idle talk. There were long walks around the little tourist town at the north end of the island, then a few hours on the beach, the sky shutting itself in with the gray insulation of clouds, the wind picking up and spraying surf and the first drops of a rainstorm. Dad, possibly a bit winded from the day's walking, waited in the car as we wound our way down the windy beach. I headed back before the rest, expecting to find my father grumpy and taciturn. Instead, I found him in the front seat of the midsize rental, contentedly listening to a Chopin nocturne on the radio. I slid in beside him, joining him in his silence, and together we looked out on the beachhead as the encroaching storm opened the clouds and transformed the sky into a dazzling light show.

BEFORE LEAVING THE apartment, I went through the pile of books still in the study. They were mostly old travel books and restaurant guides, but two books jumped out at me. One was a yellowed paperback copy of the *Kama Sutra* (the Burton translation), the other a small hardcover edition of Holbein's *The Dance of Death*, a series of sixteenth-century wood engravings depicting various ways Death comes for his victims. I slipped the two books into my backpack.

Back outside in the chill, I knew I had to pay a visit to the Cathedral of St. John the Divine. It had always been my retreat, my own private getaway when I came into the city. Since it was midday and midweek, the place was almost empty. The cavernous main hall was dark, and dusty prisms of sunlight fell from the huge stained-glass windows. I walked alongside the pews, past the AIDS memorial and the Poets' Corner, into the semicircle of small chapels. Though not an overtly religious person, I often came to these fenced-in rooms to sit at their altars. They were possibly the quietest, most meditative places I knew in the city.

But this time, in the only chapel open there was some sort of video art project on display. I leaned in to see what it was about and discovered three columnlike movie screens lined up at the altar. They spanned from floor to ceiling. The middle screen was filled with what appeared to be an angelic form floating in water. Ambient music drifted out of hidden speakers. The screen on the left showed a woman giving birth. Squatting in a chair with her husband holding her from behind, she rode through waves of contractions. Her moans blended into the ambient sound track. On the right screen, an old man lay in a hospital bed dying, his breathing shallow and erratic; the machines he was hooked up to blinked and blipped in the half-darkness of the chapel.

It took about an hour for the woman to give birth and for the old man to die. First the old man's breath stopped, then soon the baby's wails rose up and filled the room. The mother sighing and laughing in relief. Then long moments of stillness, silence. When I looked up, I saw that I had been joined by at least a dozen other people, though I had not seen or heard them come in. Overwhelmed, I went back outside and, after buying a coffee-to-go at the Hungarian bakery (Blakean paintings of angels on the walls!), headed for the airport.

In the terminal I pulled out the books from my father's apartment and leafed through them. The *Kama Sutra* instructed me on the different ways of kissing a woman, on the ways of lying, and on the different kinds of love. *The Dance of Death* showed me all the different deaths I might face. I looked for a woodcut that depicted my dad's death but couldn't find one. There was one for the judge and the priest, for the rich man and the merchant, but not for the poet.

At the end of the book there was an illustration entitled "The Fool" that depicted a man dancing with the skeleton of Death. The Fool was looking over at Death, who played the bagpipes with a quizzical, amused expression. The Fool seemed to be trying to come up with the appropriate witticism for the moment. A caption described the scene:

> The Fool holds his bladder in his hand and seems about to strike Death with it. He has put one finger in his mouth with a roguish gesture. Death is also in a gay mood; he is kicking the Fool, holding up his garment with his hand, and dancing a sprightly measure to the music of the bagpipes. The Fool is thinking out his last poor witticism before he can jest no more. Death appears to enjoy the joke.

That's how I pictured my father: sprawled out by his tub, dressed for the opera. Cuff links in place. He was dying so fast—was dead, in fact—he didn't have time to come up with the mot juste.

———

MY FATHER DIED late in 1997, the day after his fifty-fifth birthday. A few months before that, I had been offered a teaching position for the New England Literature Program's upcoming spring session. When the time came, I almost backed out, but realized the change of scene might be good for me. The long, drab Michigan winter was coming to a close, and I needed something like a New England spring. Once I arrived, the program—a six-week intensive study of literature and creative writing combined with camping, mountain climbing, and communal living—felt *too* challenging. Like the first-time camper, I just wanted to go home.

Camp Kabeyun, located on the southern tip of Lake Winnipesaukee on a hundred-acre forest preserve and bird sanctuary, was chock-full of walking trails. During that first week of staff meetings, I took whatever time I could to explore along the edge of the lake, into the forest, down by the swamp. I'd head back to my cabin early, write a quick postcard to Ali, tuck myself into my too-thin sleeping bag, and lie in the dark thinking.

I had received a letter from Jean Pedrick, a poet in her seventies who has a rich life behind her and a good life before her like a well-tended garden. She has known me since I was a boy and accepted me into her writing circle when I was fourteen. She wrote:

> I know people are telling you time will make it easier. I don't know that time makes it easier, but it gradually makes it different. You will find ways to keep him near you; reading him; or visiting his friends; and ways of moving him out of front and center, so you can get stuff done . . .

Those last words became my mantra. I repeated them as I walked down by the lake, as I prepared for my classes. *I can get stuff done.* I had work ahead of me, this next batch of days, this life to walk through.

Finally, after days of preparation, the students arrived. One after the other, white university vans pulled into camp. Bleary-eyed college students piled out, shell-shocked from the two-day drive, asking questions, lugging backpacks, and looking around at the campground. And just like that my solitary world—my own private spa—exploded into a whirlwind of start-up activities, group meetings, and cleanup crews.

Most days I was too busy to tell if I was doing okay or not: staff got up early and didn't stop moving until well past midnight. After the first few days of orientation, we began teaching courses on Emerson, Thoreau, Dickinson, and Frost. Journal groups began meeting, creative writing workshops formed. There were a few times when I could get away by myself, free to walk along the lake's edge for an hour, poke around in the flotsam, or sit on one of the big rocks above Panther Beach. In such quiet moments I'd often find myself close to tears. The hard fact of my father's death never left me, but its clutch on my heart was loosening. Calls home to Ali helped, but there was no hiding it: I was a wreck.

The grief I had been dodging and bracing for finally caught up to me, disguised in the form of a young student in need of help. One young woman had just learned of her best friend's mother's sudden death. I walked with Pamela, listening to her story, giving assurance. When we finally joined a gathering of concerned students, I told her, "You're in shock now, expect the grief to show up later."

Then I walked on, back to my own duties, and as I thought of Pamela, whom I didn't really know yet, I wished her well. That's when the tears came. Like a sudden storm. I didn't want to give in so kept walking along the outskirts of the camp, crying and shaking. Twenty minutes later, I was still crying; it was time for lunch and I didn't want to be crying, so I went in to get food. The tears dried up while I filled my plate, but as soon as I sat down they came back, and I sat there in the corner crying. Eventually, a group of students, including Pamela, came over and comforted me. Now it was my turn to be protected by the safety net of near strangers. It felt good. I wanted even more to be in my partner's arms, but this would do.

DURING THE PROGRAM, Walter Clark, one of the original founders of NELP and a retired professor from the Residential College at the University of Michigan, asked me to join him for walks in the woods. We went out walking no more than three times, and never for more than half an hour, an hour. The walks would begin nonchalantly, with Walter drifting over to my table at dinner to note the quality of light outside, or by answering my question about the trails around the back of Heron's Swamp with a nod of the head and a quiet "I'll be ready right after supper." Only once did we stray from the meandering road, only once slipping into the forest of pines, birches, and beeches, out past Walter's tent and down toward the lake. Nevertheless, in my mind, these walks stand out as a turning point in my time at NELP and in my dealings with my father's death.

Walter was a poet himself and had read and admired my father's work, so I think he understood something of what it was like to be the son of a celebrated poet, to stand in his shade. He asked very few questions, but each one was right on the mark. He asked what it was like dealing with all the old students, friends, and lovers. And I remember thinking, *How'd he know?*

Over the last six months, I had been besieged by dozens of letters and calls. At first, and for the most part, receiving these messages, this inpouring of sympathy and grief, helped my family and me make sense of his sudden death. (As one friend put it, "In the literary world, lighting up the phone lines is maybe the biggest compliment.") After a while, however, I began to feel suffocated by the barrage of words—of praise, of grief, of consolation. They were heartwarming and overwhelming, curative and poisoning. It felt like my duty as a "good" son to field them all. Walter urged me to disconnect myself, and he seemed relieved that I had already begun to. *You need time for your own soul, for your own emotions*, he told me. And he had been right.

Just as we were making our way back into camp on that first walk, Walter had stressed how good a fit he thought NELP and I made. It had come as a surprise. For though I had been giving everything I had—volunteering for extra duties, jumping into new experiences right along with the students—I felt out of sync with the NELPers and a few steps behind the other staffers. I don't know if Walter had seen this and was just offering me encouragement, or if he genuinely meant it, but his words gave me welcome confidence in myself and in my work.

During the two weeks of his visit, Walter rarely held forth, joining in discussion lightly with a well-placed question or a fresh insight. He cooked bread for the meals, showing how to prepare the starter batch; he could be found, as well, nearly every morning out chopping at the woodpile. I don't know if the students fully understood who he was, or what he was doing there. But, for sure, when he left, heading back to his nearby summer house, they sensed his absence.

The night Walter left I met fellow staffers Sam and Sean at a bonfire down at Panther Beach. A few of the young male students had drums and were quietly braiding half-familiar West African rhythms into a song. I had just come back from a long walk with a student in my journal group. During our ramble, Joe had talked about his dad, expressing both his love for him and his impatience. At some point in the walk, I caught myself bending my head the way Walter had done with me—all the better to pick up the nuances. It felt good to be listening. Now, as Joe rolled us Drum cigarettes, I took out my journal and set to work on a poem about my walks with Walter.

With a few changes, here's what I wrote:

WALKING WITH WALTER
    for my father

Walter wants to know how I'm doing
so far, what I think of this and that.
It's a simple gift to be in the beam
of Walter's interest. And there's something
of the dignitary in Walter's way
with people, cross-bred as it is with the absent mind
of the professor and the sure hand of the gentleman
farmer (straight out of some lesser-known
Frost poem). A soul emissary, then, who
at present—as we pass up through
the burgeoning pines, along a New England

stone wall—is asking about my father,
recently dead, about how it has been
dealing with the aftermath and all
the troubled souls that end up at the door
of the dead poet's house uninvited.
He seems to understand: brother, father,
teacher—yes, even son. He's that good
at listening. And listening, too, for some echo
out of the forest, some crow flap to awaken
an answer (in me?). He just nods. We keep walking
and as we go forward, me conjuring my
love for my father, I feel some hidden part
dislodge, take wing, fly up
to join the crow in the late afternoon haze—
my body moving onward with Walter, as light
as cumulus clouds passing soundlessly over water.

After All

Love needs to be set alight
again and again, and in thanks
for tending it, will do its very
best not to consume it.

WILLIAM MATTHEWS, "Care"

November 11, 2002

T HIS MORNING I scan my face in the bathroom mirror for signs of my father. The slowly receding hairline is there, along with the "sophisticated" gray at the temples. The wear of living life shows up under my eyes the way it did for him. It's like that Donald Justice poem about middle age: my face is gradually filling in with the image of my father. It makes me wonder if maybe the truest inheritance of all resides in the body: the tight hips, the wrecked knees, the questionable heart wired to blow, its slow-burning fuse already lit. Today is my father's birthday. If he were still alive, he'd be sixty. I turned thirty-seven a few months ago. Looking up from this busy life, I realize my father has been dead now for five years.

It's hard to believe that Ali and I uprooted our lives in Ann Arbor more than three years ago and moved down here to Asheville, North Carolina; that we have been teaching at this small progressive college in the mountains long enough for my first freshman writing student to be graduating. I can still remember how, after a year in campus housing, we bought and moved into this house. Remember waking up late one of our first nights in the house, disoriented, needing to piss. The hall was dark and I had to make a trail of unsure steps to the faraway light. Finally I give up, throw out my hands, and walk, fingertips running along the freshly painted walls, the last few yards to open door.

We had to keep assuring ourselves that all we needed was a little time to settle in. And, of course, we did gradually settle, finding a rhythm in our lives by making new friends and discovering places we liked to go and the local routes to get there, by busying ourselves with the usual tasks that come with home ownership—hauling and cleaning, stripping and painting, decorating and landscaping. And there were dinner parties, hiking trips, visits from family. Things work out. Owning this house helped: it gave us something to attach ourselves to. It helped, too, that Asheville has its share of good restaurants, coffee shops, and bookstores. When we were particularly homesick for Ann Arbor, we could go and sit at Beanstreets, a downtown coffeehouse, and read the *New York Times*.

My daily walks on the nearby public golf course with our new dog, a chocolate Lab named Ursula, once in the morning and once at dusk, provided a nice counterbalance to time in the classroom and at the desk. Ali quickly found herself happy in her job at Warren Wilson College, excited to be teaching and surprised by her growing involvement in the school's day-to-day operations. She planted an herb garden (another sure sign of settling), and, when we remembered to, we picked basil and mint and rosemary to add taste to our dinners.

Only my writing seemed to have stalled. Month after month, I left my father's old desk propped up in the center of the room surrounded by boxes of books. (The movers snapped off one of its legs in the unloading, so now it needs a filing cabinet to lean on.) The best I could manage was to carve out a few hours for writing. Nothing consistent, never very focused. Finally, upon Ali's urging, I purchased bookcases and spent a weekend filling the shelves with books. If I couldn't write, at least I could create a writing space.

The trick worked, for slowly I fell into a routine, getting up early in the mornings and sitting down at my desk. A sketch here, a poem there. Before I knew it, I was writing again, although it took a while to recognize it as such. Eventually I was writing about my father's death. How, when he died suddenly, it felt like being turned around in a sharp wind. How, in many ways, he had become the Minotaur in my maze, everywhere and nowhere at once. It was all strangely cathartic, as if writing about the facts of his death helped me recover from it. Over time, a portrait of my father—of my relationship to him—rose to the surface, a negative in its pan of developer.

No heralding trumpets, though. Usually after about an hour, I'd be lost, stripped of the energy to go further. It wasn't for lack of material, of course, more a hesitancy on my part to dig deep. Now that I was actively looking for my father, there was much to be unsure about. The harder I tried, the less I fathomed the mixed legacy he had left me. How could I hold up all the positives when they came tethered to so many negatives?

At first, I wanted simply to pry open the shut box of memory. If I could accomplish that, I told myself, then maybe I would be free of some of this confusion that, like a stubborn houseguest, seemed to have taken up residence in my body. This morning, for instance, I work on a sketch that comes from one of my earliest childhood memories. It's of my father's body. He is naked in the tub, sharing a bath with my brother and me. There's a reddish pink birthmark on his chest and stomach. In the shape of France, he tells us, pointing out where different wines and cheeses are made. Later, I'll go into the kitchen and look up at the poster of France, trying to make the connection.

Happy with the couple of paragraphs I have produced, I close the computer down. Propped up behind the keyboard is the birthday card I sent to my father and reclaimed from his apartment. My glance falls on a highlighted passage:

A year ago, I was really worried about you. I wondered about your health. But I don't worry anymore. You seem to be doing quite well.

Here was the dutiful son telling his soon-to-be-dead father he's looking well. But I have come to view it differently. Now when I read it, I know I am also talking to myself.

Ursula is insisting that I take her out. No argument from me. We settle into a long walk around the neighborhood, cutting across the golf course's back nine. When we return home, I am winded and happy, not yet ready to return to the desk. I start to wander around our house, instead, passing from room to room. I am struck by how—in a weird, 3-D version of time-lapse photography—we have transformed this house from empty shell into cozy home. How, in a few short months, we have the house feeling lived in. A new couch appears magically in the living room. A fresh coat of paint washes the walls. The poster print gracing the kitchen with just the right blue. Our new friends remark on how fast we settled in. We are the first to admit it: the more our living space feels lived in, we figure, the more we can begin our new lives.

Looking around this house now, I might be tempted to say that our life here is brand new. A slate wiped clean. Of course, nothing could be further from the truth. The ghosts of that former time have made the journey south. They're in the furniture I have inherited, in the rows of his old jazz albums, in the hardcover books, the artwork on the walls, the desk at which I write. And in the very walls themselves, for the family money that came down through my father enabled us to buy this house. Indeed, my life has been built on the ruins, and the spoils, of the past.

I wear my father's inherited loves as emotional hand-me-downs. Now when I put on a Lester Young record or crack open a reference book or sit down at my desk, I evoke my father. I wear his old sweater in a dumb, corporeal prayer. The same is true in the kitchen: the omelette Ali prepared this morning was cooked in my father's seasoned pan, the soup I concocted the other night was his recipe and stirred by one of his scarred wooden spoons. These chipped dishes I put in the sink are his; I clean them to ground myself and to kill time.

Iᴛ ᴡᴀs ɪᴍᴘᴏʀᴛᴀɴᴛ to my father that I know how to make a good risotto. A risotto is classy comfort food, he once said, either a bachelor's salvage job or a couple's therapy. Before you begin the hot work over the stove, you must prepare yourself and your ingredients. First and foremost, making a risotto grounds the cook at the stove. You will be allowed only brief forays to the fridge or spice rack before having to return to the job at hand: the ever-present stirring at the heart of any good risotto. You must always take your time, he admonished. Risottos can never be rushed.

My father started the night's work by opening a good bottle of wine. He would keep a glass close at hand as he cut up vegetables. He'd grate the Parmesan, select his spices, pausing to take sniffs of the freshly uncorked bottle. If he was adding meat—sausage or prosciutto—he would first cook it on the side, maybe fry up the veggies lightly in olive oil. Mushrooms and peppers were good. Garlic. Fresh basil. Whatever fit his taste that night or whatever he had in the fridge.

Another custom: put on good music. Music that fills you up with a quiet happiness and animates your movements. If it's an Indian summer, open the windows. My father would invite friends to come early so he could tell them the special stories behind the vintage of the wine he was pouring, then shoo them from the kitchen so he could get back to work. He was the night's mooring; the risotto was his anchor.

Tonight, it's Ali cutting the onion, making sure to chop the pieces fine. I drizzle a generous amount of olive oil in the bottom of one of Dad's good-size cooking pots. Over medium flame, I "mate" the oil and onions with a pinch of salt. After a minute, remembering my father's instructions, I throw in two or three big handfuls of arborio rice, stirring vigorously for about a minute. The point here is to let the rice crack open. (*The better to receive the flavor, my dear.*)

As you stir risotto, you must remember to keep ladling the warmed stock into the rice. It's important that you spoon in small amounts—somewhere between an eighth and a quarter of a cup, but you can eyeball it—and then gently stir the liquid into the rice. Why? Because the rice is releasing its wonderful starches, my father would remind me, and we are here to encourage a new equilibrium. And he'd sip from his glass, for he, too, was achieving a new balance. Which gets me thinking of the toast I want to propose at dinner in my father's honor. I am not yet sure what I'll say, but just in case, I've copied down a line from one of my father's interviews: "A world in which I cannot share another meal with my father is a diminished one."

Ali takes over at the stove, spooning in more stock while I flip the disc (James Taylor's *Greatest Hits*) and turn up the music. The waft of onion mixes with the breeze from the open door. After about half an hour, or when the rice has swelled up and started to get mushy, just past al dente, I fold in the meat and veggies in batches with the stock. Ali tosses a little of the Parmesan into the mix and sets the table.

One of the tricks to risotto I learned by watching my father is to add in extra stock near the end so that the rice becomes a soup. I turn up the heat a little and step away from the stove. For a few moments I am free to move around. I can step outside, use the bathroom, change the music. (Maybe one of the Desmond/Hall recordings or the Cowboy Junkies.) I return to the stove before the risotto begins sticking to the pan.

Now the risotto is almost ready. A few last ladles, maybe a little more cheese, some fresh-ground pepper. The bowls are sitting by the stove, waiting for me to spoon in the sticky rice. I open a bottle I know my father would have approved of—a spicy red from Umbria—and fill our glasses. On the table: sparkling water in sweaty glasses, brittle-crusted bread in a basket, a small dish of olives. Ali's put together a salad topped with cucumbers, almonds, dried cherries. She lights candles and turns off the lights.

Near the end of my father's last book of poems, *After All*, there's a poem about cooking. In it, my father says to his love:

> *it's far too late*
> *to unlove each other. Instead let's cook*
> *something elaborate and not*
> *invite anyone to share it but eat it*
> *all up very very slowly.*

Though he doesn't say what it is they're cooking, I know it is risotto. When you take up something your parent loved, you are both spending and cultivating your inheritance.

∿

THE OTHER NIGHT I dreamed that my father was driving my brother and me along a country back road in our old humpbacked Volvo. We were apparently on a vacation trip, for the car was brimming over with suitcases and goodwill. My father seemed especially excited to get to where we were going and so drove happily, one hand free to punctuate the running monologue he'd been performing for us. When we passed into the fringes of town, coming up to and then cresting the small gap in the mountains, a beautiful valley opened up before us. And though I didn't recognize it, I knew right away that we had returned to my birthplace, Chapel Hill, North Carolina, the site of my father's graduate school years. I turned to smile at my father, to thank him for bringing me back, but he was crying. With both hands on the wheel, head bowed, he was bawling like a baby.

The dream reminds me of a poem my mother sent me earlier this year. A poem, surprisingly, about my father. In it, she and Charter are out in their sailboat, heading up the coast of Maine for a weekend jaunt. It's a true story. They lay anchor in a little cove and, after looking at the map, my mom realizes they are in the cove my father used to summer in with his old writing buddies. The poem's called "Mackerel Sky Elegy," and here is how it ends:

Now I remember: At the funeral, men with cropped silver hair and flecked beards told stories about that summer place. How they gave each other nicknames and drank good wine and smoked fine cigars. Oh, how they laughed.

How they remembered you.

From this vantage, anchored in the very cove you and your friends must have overlooked from a porch on warm foggy evenings long after you and I had anything left to say to one another, I can almost

see you, as if through a screen. In profile. Cigarette in one hand,
snifter in the other. Holding forth. You seem at ease, even happy.
Then suddenly, peripherally, you notice me. Momentarily taken
aback, the surface of your composure fractures like moonlight on a
windy bay. But you neither turn nor move away. You must sense
that I'm only here for this evening with no intention of startling.
And I . . .

This must be why I have come. To say goodby.

My mother has been happy in her life with Charter, far removed
from that first marriage, so it is strange, and touching, to hear her
say goodbye to my father. For years, under a child's illusion, I've
thought of them as inhabiting different worlds. But they were
actually a lot alike, and bound together by the past, and by their
children. They *were* each other's first loves, after all. My mother's
story helps me make sense of the dream: for it was Chapel Hill
where their marriage first started souring, the place where our family life began to fracture.

Soon Mom and Charter will be coming to visit us in our new
house. Ali and I are excited to show off our life here in Asheville.
It's been over a year since they last made the trip. In that time, my
mom has been named Poet Laureate of New Hampshire. With four
books out and a fifth on the way, and with her longtime work in
the state's libraries and schools, she deserves it.

In a few months I will fly out to Seattle to spend time with my
brother and his family. His two oldest kids have grown up, one
already off to college. The two younger ones are blossoming swiftly
into their lives. Much of the sibling rivalry between Bill and me

has burned off; now we are left with mutual good feeling. We are veterans of our own childhood, bound together for life by the experience.

Ali and I are going to her parents' for Passover. There are even plans to meet Mary and Susan Matthews in Ireland for a summer vacation. We will rent a car and drive up the west coast together, visiting coastal towns to scout out traditional music in the pubs. It feels good to be so connected to family.

I have lost touch with Celia, though. Our family has. Distance grew between us soon after the divisions of my father's things. There were a few phone calls, a long letter. Maybe it is better this way. I think I wanted Celia to be my father's savior the way, as a boy, I wanted Sharon to be my stepmom.

While I'm at it, I want my father back. In my life and in his. But since he's gone and I am more or less able, there is work to be done. I wouldn't have chosen this work because I'd not have chosen his death. But here I am: back in his garden, weeding again. In one busy week, I have given permission for two poem reprints, started proofing a book of his essays and interviews, and begun gathering together unpublished poems for his *Collected*.

I am proud of my father's work and don't mind serving as stand-in gardener; I have even learned to appreciate the labor, the way it instructs me about the necessary hardships of life, the simple cause-and-effect economics of work. Indeed, a new literary life has bloomed out of the scorched earth. For now I keep in abundant— and from their end, generous—touch with my father's old writing buddies, as well as with a good number of his students, teaching colleagues, and well-wishers. Together we serve as stewards of my father's legacy, both as poet and teacher.

It dawns on me now that in my father's last years he and I unexpectedly wound up on the same track of transformation: both of us finding partners with whom to settle, staying in one place for more than a few years. It was as if the roles were reversed, and all of a sudden my father seemed to be looking at my marriage with Ali—and the stability I had found with her—as something to strive for. I became, in some small way and for a short time, his role model for a new life. But now any forward progress he may or may not have been making has been halted. It's just me, left to hold the bags of memory.

My father said in an interview that "the mysteries that lie in childhood are continually reinvented as we go through life remembering them." Believing this is true, I launch myself over and over into the reservoir of memory. Each time I dive, I hope to go deep. Each time I come up for air, I hope to emerge new.

Acknowledgments

I would like to thank Russell Banks, Charles Baxter, and Nicholas Delbanco for serving as my mentors—on this book and in my writing life. I would also like to thank Bob Reiss, Judith Kitchen, Peter Davison, and Barry Sanders for their invaluable guidance and support at various stages of this project.

Numerous friends and colleagues have helped me along the way. I would like to thank in particular Luke Bergmann, Howell Burnell, Elizabeth Clark, Dr. Lawrence Climo, Margot Livesey, Paula McLain, Chase Twichell, and Emilie White for reading drafts of this work and providing much-needed insight and encouragement.

Thanks also to my readers and teachers at the University of Michigan, the Bread Loaf Writers' Conference, and Vermont Studio Center. Special thanks to Marie Harris, my mother and fellow writer, who let me tell my version of the story; to Alison Climo, my wife, to whom this book is dedicated, for all her help and support; to Charter Weeks for being such an amazing father; to all the friends and colleagues of William Matthews, who generously filled in blanks and let me retell some of their stories; and to all my students and friends for helping keep me honest.

Lastly, I would like to thank my agent, Diana Finch, for sticking with me, and Carol Houck Smith, editor extraordinaire, who took a chance on a not-so-young writer still learning the ropes. I couldn't have done it without you.

Parts of this book appeared, in slightly different versions, in *Atlantic Monthly*, *Brilliant Corners*, the *Virginia Quarterly Review*, *Parabola*, *Paragraph*, and *Tin House*.

Thanks go to Cynthia Atkins, Marvin Bell, Sharon Bryan, Sascha Feinstein, Gayle Hummel, Rick Jackson, and Jean Pedrick for sharing portions of their letters and e-mails. The excerpts from an unidentified interview with William Matthews come from the radio program *New Letters on the Air*.

I have changed a few names in this memoir for the sake of privacy.

Permission Credits

The author is grateful for permission to reprint:

A line from "The Moose," from *Standup Comic* by Woody Allen. Copyright © 1978 by Tyrell Music Group. Reprinted by permission of Rhino Records.

"The Same River Twice," from *Salt Air* (Wesleyan University Press). Copyright © 1983 by Sharon Bryan. Reprinted by permission of Sharon Bryan.

A line from "Idiot Wind," from *Blood on the Tracks* by Bob Dylan. Copyright © 1974 by Ram's Horn Music. Reprinted by permission of Ram's Horn Music. All rights reserved.

"Cooking the Rat" by Charles Gaines, from *Fathers & Sons*. Copyright © 1992 by David Seybold. Reprinted by permission of Grove Weidenfeld.

"Mackerel Sky" by Marie Harris. Copyright © 2002. Reprinted by permission of Marie Harris.

An excerpt from *The Dance of Death* by Hans Holbein. Copyright © 1947 by Phaidon Press Ltd. Reprinted by permission of Oxford University Press.